Take Control

of

Your Anxiety

A DRUG-FREE APPROACH TO
LIVING A HAPPY, HEALTHY LIFE

TAKE
CONTROL
OF YOUR
ANXIETY

DR. CHRIS CORTMAN,
DR. HAROLD SHINITZKY, AND
DR. LAURIE-ANN O'CONNOR

CAREER
PRESS

Pompton Plains, NJ

TAKE CONTROL OF YOUR ANXIETY
EDITED BY GINA SCHENCK
TYPESET BY EILEEN MUNSON
Cover design by Rob Johnson
Printed in the U.S.A.

To order this title, please call toll-free 1-800-CAREER-1 (NJ and Canada: 201-848-0310) to order using VISA or MasterCard, or for further information on books from Career Press.

The Career Press, Inc.
220 West Parkway, Unit 12
Pompton Plains, NJ 07444
www.careerpress.com

Library of Congress Cataloging-in-Publication Data
Cortman, Christopher.
  Take control of your anxiety : a drug-free approach to living a happy, healthy life /
by Dr. Christopher Cortman, Dr. Harold Shinitzky, and Dr. Laurie-Ann O'Connor.
-- 1
      pages cm
Includes bibliographical references and index.
  ISBN 978-1-60163-356-9 (paperback) -- ISBN 978-1-60163-404-7 (ebook) 1.
Anxiety. 2. Anxiety disorders. 3. Self-help techniques. I. Shinitzky, Harold. II.
O'Connor, Laurie-Ann. III. Title.

BF575.A6C667 2015
152.4'6--dc23

                                                                    2014045652

Acknowledgments

Christopher

I would like to dedicate this book to my lovely wife Stephanie, who in the midst of a mastectomy and extremely aggressive chemotherapy and radiation, supported me and my efforts to write this book. Never once did she complain about my weekends at Barnes & Noble, nor my meetings with my two coauthors. Only once did she agree with me when I suggested that we sell our three young children on eBay. Stephanie, you are a warrior, a role model, and a very competent human being. I'm proud of you for all you have done and are doing. As a result, I dedicate this book to you and every woman grappling with the formidable foe of breast cancer.

I would also like to thank Bruce W. for his many insights and generosity, Lisa the Barnes & Noble unofficial editor, Andrea for her helpful comments and support, and most of all, my patients who have supplied me with more insights and wisdom than any university or college ever could. Thank you for trusting me with your lives and may all of you benefit from our work and this book.

Finally, I'd like to thank my children, Cameron, Melina, and Dylan, all of whom sacrificed time with daddy so that I could get this project completed on time. I love you kids more than you will ever understand, until you become parents yourselves.

Harold

I would like to thank my supervisors and colleagues at the Johns Hopkins University School of Medicine for encouraging me to strive to be my best. They emphasized that medication was never the primary intervention. Behavioral interventions were always primary. I would like to thank my family and friends for their support even when I disappeared to write this manuscript. In particular, I would like to thank Teresa for her love, understanding that Sunday nights were with Chris and L.A., and her honesty to intellectually challenge concepts that helped expand key points throughout the book. Lastly, I would like to thank my patients for educating me on their daily personal struggles and experiences with anxiety. By working collaboratively with them toward achieving their goals made my work professionally and personally very rewarding.

Laurie-Ann

Many thanks to Chris and Harold for the opportunity to be a coauthor of this book. It was both an honor and a pleasure to join you in this work. I also thank Dr. Bob Boxley for his advice and years of guidance. Finally, I am grateful for the many people who have shared their stories, lives, and pain with me. You have all taught me more than you know.

We would like to thank Laurie Kelly-Pye, Michael Pye, Adam Schwartz, and all of the great people at Career Press for appreciating the value of addressing the important issue of anxiety.

Contents

Introduction

There must be 17,632 books on anxiety. So why another one? *Time* magazine recently declared that anxiety has two faces: "it can paralyze you—or help you move faster. New science is revealing more about the upside of angst."[1] But to the rest of us, when the race is to make it to dinnertime without losing our tempers, jobs, or minds over the stressors we juggle, anxiety is no friend.

Anxiety disorders are the new common cold of mental illness, replacing depression as the most oft-diagnosed emotional disorder. The world is faster paced, more complicated, more diverse, and more competitive than ever. It's virtually impossible to traverse your 80 or more years of life without experiencing an overload of anxiety symptoms at some point, which brings me to the next point: this book is not only for the 18.1 percent of Americans suffering from an anxiety disorder. It's also for the other 81.9 percent of Americans who are experiencing subclinical (normal) symptoms of anxiety, like you.[2]

What I have attempted to create is a book that is entirely readable and informative—edutainment, if you will—to help you understand and *take control of your anxiety*. (Note the clever inclusion of the book title.) I aim to help you become a more knowledgeable, healthy, and high-functioning individual after reading this book by applying the principles, doing the exercises, and practicing new thinking styles and techniques. Change requires effort and you may need to make some changes.

The stories and examples are real and are included to serve as helpful illustrations as to how the principles, techniques, and tools work. Some of these may be more helpful to you than others. Your results may vary, however, I want you to know that there is hope, even for "hopelessly anxious" you.

I will stay in the first person throughout the book despite the contributions of three authors. (If you like the writing style, credit Dr. Cortman. If not, blame Drs. Shinitzky and O'Connor.)

Another thing: we do not talk much about medication in the book. Why not? As psychologists, we owe you the understanding and knowledge of 100-ish years of psychological science that can help you to *take control of your anxiety* (there it is again). Finally, we are pleased to inform you that the research has repeatedly confirmed that the very best treatments for *all* anxiety disorders are psychologic, not psychotropic (medication).

Don't get me wrong. I am not anti-medication and definitely not anti-psychiatrist. But let me make this point: if you are taking medication for anxiety without any other type of help, you are *not* doing everything you can for your issues. So thank you for buying my book. Now go buy one for your physician.

1 Understanding Anxiety

If stress burns calories, I'd be a super model.

—Unknown

Scott's Story

Scott was anxious—*really* anxious. He hadn't slept a wink in three nights and somehow still had the energy to pace about the room and plan his own funeral. He wasn't suicidal; he was just imagining the various methods his father might use to arrange a meeting between Scott and his maker as soon as Dad heard the news.

You see, Scott was the first person in the history of his family to attend college and yet, here he was three years later awaiting possible expulsion for an embarrassing infraction.

He hadn't eaten since the incident. He was not allowed access to the cafeteria for a full week after the spectacle last Thursday. Besides, with all the anxiety, he just wasn't hungry. He looked awful: bloodshot eyes, preternatural wrinkles across his brow, and a look that conveyed an emotion somewhere between torture and terror.

It began innocently enough: Henry, Gary, and Scott enjoying another leisurely lunch together in the school cafeteria. Scott called Henry a "pea brain" after fielding a playful insult from his good buddy. "A pea brain," Henry laughed mockingly, and calmly loaded his spoon with a bunch of peas from his plate. Waiting until the perfect moment, Henry fired his peas across the table and into Scott's face. His aim was perfect, peas bouncing off Scott's head in all directions. One rogue pea, evidently laced with mashed potatoes, stuck to Scott's glasses directly in front of his right pupil. Everyone laughed, of course, and Henry, feeling victorious after his successful launch, could only ask, "So who's the *pea* brain, Scott?"

Scott felt emasculated, needless to say. He should have laughed along with the others and left it at that. But 21-year-old wisdom is often contaminated by testosterone, which cries out for vengeance. Not to be defeated, he loaded up his spoon—his mashed potatoes were soaked with gravy—and fired them as hard as he could at Henry's smirk. But Henry predictably ducked, and the starch-packed missile sailed to the next table and thumped Betty Evans, dean of students, directly in the back of her perfectly coiffed beehive. Scott's jaw dropped as his blood pressure skyrocketed—this could not be good!

If Scott was embarrassed by his errant toss, Dean Evans was humiliated by the laughter and attention from the carbo-load in her hair and gravy on her neck. And whatever possessed Gary, the third musketeer, to eat potatoes off the Dean's pink cashmere sweater, remains a mystery. The boys were to meet at her office the following morning at "O nine hundred hours! And no cafeteria privileges for a week!" She stomped out of a now quiet, stunned cafeteria, leaving the young men to ponder what was left of their future at this conservative institution.

It's never good to assault a Dean. It's arguably worse to publicly humiliate her. But when she resorted to yelling about private meetings on military time schedules in a non-military school, well, the boys knew their geese were cooked. But the following morning produced three anguished young men and no Dean Evans. The note on her door only stated, "Gentleman. There has been a death in my family. Meet here 6 p.m. Wed. Do *not* be late!"

On Wednesday night, it was Dean Evans who was late, 17 minutes, to be exact. She maintained her stern look, nary a smile, and said only, "Follow me." The boys trailed her single file, like ducklings behind their fast-paced momma, out a side door and into the dark, cool November evening. At 6:30 they arrived at a nearby house, Dean Evans's home, for the biggest surprise of their lives. A small banquet was prepared for them, including roast beef, biscuits, and of course, peas, but with baked potatoes! "You might not want to launch these, Scott, they're loaded with sour cream and butter, not instant, like that cafeteria crap!" The widowed Dean Evans admitted, "Every night I feel guilty about you three idiots starving to death—this was the least I could do to make it up to you. Now eat up and learn a life lesson!"

To hear Scott tell it years later, there were numerous life lessons to be gathered and shared for the rest of his life: "First, there must be a force who saved people from the consequences of stupid decisions. Secondly, forgiveness is alive and well and more powerful than anything in the universe, except for love. Finally, worry, dread, and anxiety are self-created wastes of emotional energy. I've learned to replace them with hope, faith, and positive thinking."

He then added one more pearl of wisdom: always choose baked over instant.

xxx

Ever wonder what really goes on behind the closed doors of a psychologist's office? Ever think you could relate to the issues patients are sharing?

Lest you should still be holding on to the antiquated belief that mental health professionals treat "crazy" people, let me share the highlights of a clinical psychologist's typical day.

> A 60-year-old woman has been married to an excessively controlling professional man for the past 32 years. She becomes anxious when her husband calls her into the den to "discuss" last month's credit card statement. She would like to change all that control, but is petrified to stir up the waters.

> An 80-year-old woman, a mother of four sons, makes her initial visit with the following complaint: "My son, Greg, committed suicide two years ago. I thought I was going to be alright...truth be told, I can't stop obsessing about it and can't sleep worth a damn..."

- ☒ An 8-year-old boy hears noises outside his bedroom window so he is afraid to sleep alone. During the day, he readily admits he knows the sounds come from the tree branches scratching against the window pane. Nevertheless, he still panics every night.

- ☒ A 47-year-old man, referred by his physician after noting a spike in blood pressure, complains that his life as a financial planner has become overwhelming with the economic downturn. He lives in fear of disappointing and losing his clients...and his job.

- ☒ A 14-year-old boy refuses to return to school. Long a favorite target of two of the high school's most notorious bullies, he feels ridiculed and ashamed and vows never to "show his face in that class again."

- ☒ A 30-year-old professional athlete avoids flying because he is afraid the plane will crash. Instead, he takes a bus or a train to his game and is embarrassed when his teammates razz him.

- ☒ A 13-year-old girl panics at the thought of getting back into her mom's SUV after the vehicle was hit on her side of the car a week prior.

- ☒ A 41-year-old man, a survivor of childhood sexual abuse, drinks himself to sleep each night in an effort to shut off the intrusive flashbacks of his victimization. He'd like to quit drinking if he could just get "those memories to go away."

This is one clinical day among many throughout the year. And what do these patients have in common? Each one of them is manifesting symptoms of an anxiety disorder, conditions that mental health professionals are diagnosing and treating with more and more frequency. In fact, anxiety disorders are now considered to be the common cold of mental disorders, replacing mood disorders (depression) as the most prevalent.

In a study of 26,000 subjects in 14 countries, it was found that physical disability was more closely associated with psychological factors than it was with medical.[1]

So how do people succumb to an anxiety disorder? Are they born with it? Is it the result of poor upbringing? A traumatic experience? Is an anxiety disorder a life sentence or is it treatable? Does it necessitate treatment with tranquilizers or other medications? I will stop bombarding you with questions and promise to address them in the pages ahead. But for now...let's turn our attention to understanding anxiety.

What Is Anxiety?

The root meaning of the word *anxiety* is "to vex or trouble." Anxiety is a psychological and physiological state (mind and body) associated with feelings of fear, worry, uneasiness, dread, or nervousness. Although a certain degree of anxiety is a normal part of life, when it occurs too often, too severely, or is unmanageable, anxiety can be classified as a disorder.

Investment + Threat = Anxiety

Anxiety begins in your brain when you perceive a threat to your world. The threat can be to your life, such as a hurricane, rape, or mugging, but most often, anxiety is spawned by threats of a non-fatal nature, such as the imminent threat of job termination, relationship breakup, or court date. Any of these situations, if perceived to be a threat, has the power to create symptoms of anxiety just as intense as if they were life-threatening. Sometimes, as you will see in Chapter 3, anxiety is nothing more than a vague sense of dread regarding the unknown aspects of the road ahead. Anxiety is always about the future and, again, always sends a message of threat.

There is a second component to the creation of the feelings of anxiety: investment. Anxiety never occurs without investment, that is, caring about someone or something. If the job means nothing because there are other options, expect little or no anxiety about losing it. If, however, school represents the world to you, then each and every exam may have the power to create a maelstrom of nerves and apprehension. As I wrote in the first chapter of *Your Mind: An Owner's Manual for a Better Life*, Investment + Threat = Anxiety.

No situation or person causes stress or anxiety. What is stressful to you may not create stress in someone else. Your emotion of anxiety is a statement about you, for example, losing a job may be devastating to one individual but freeing to another.

To wit, I never cared about the local Babe Ruth baseball team until my nephew played for them. The stock market didn't even exist for me until I invested my first $1,000 after college. The cost of preschool was completely irrelevant and non-consequential before I had my first toddler. *Grecian Formula* commercials were of little interest, until gray hairs invaded my temples. Without investment there will be no anxiety, and without the perception of threat to that investment, there will be no anxiety. Think about it. Every anxiety-inducing situation in your life—the boss's perception of your project, your granddaughter's piano recital, your wife's biopsy—all produce anxiety in you only because you are invested in the outcome.

Why is that so important to understand? If anxiety can be traced back to your investments and threats, you can learn to think and respond differently to every anxiety-inducing situation and relationship in your life. The potential for situations that evoke anxiety are endless: cheerleading try-outs, a physician with a blood pressure cuff, a late-night visit from a cockroach in the kitchen, flashing police lights in your rear-view mirror, news of breast cancer, an ominous storm report from the Weather Channel, and so on. What do these situations have in common? Each may represent a potential threat to some aspect of your life, and if the situation is important to you (investment) and you perceive an imminent danger (threat), you will experience symptoms of anxiety.

According to Behavioral Medicine Associates of Atlanta and Alpharetta, Georgia, anxiety symptoms include a feeling of impending doom, that one is losing his or her mind or is about to faint, collapse, have a seizure or die of a heart attack or stroke. Physical symptoms include rapid and pounding heartbeat, pulsing arteries especially in the head or neck, shortness of breath, hyperventilation, trembling, sweating, generalized bodily weakness, and lightheadedness. Still other symptoms of anxiety include paresthesia (tingling sensations in the extremities), choking, and tightness and/or pain in the chest.[2]

But, change either part of the equation, the investment or the threat, and the entire picture changes immediately. Let's reexamine the previous examples, but this time we will alter one aspect of each situation. Your best friend tells you she is certain the coach likes you and you are "sure to make the squad." The doctor tells you your blood pressure was perfect for your age so there's no concern. Your husband says, "Go back to the bedroom. That roach is mine!" As you pull over, the police cruiser continues his hot pursuit of some other driver. You learn that the breast cancer survival rate is high and that your prognosis is much better than you had anticipated. Your wife reminds you that in a storm your family is invited to stay with friends who live in a safer location and the rest of it is just "stuff" anyway.

If you check the examples one more time, note that anxiety was reduced by removing or reducing the perception of threat in every situation but the last one. In the final scenario, the perception of threat remained the same—the weather was still ominous—but the investment changed when it was decided that the house and the contents therein amounted only to "stuff," and was, therefore, replaceable.

Understanding the formula of *investment + threat* is essential for the chronically anxious person to completely reconstruct the thinking patterns that tend routinely to create anxiety. In fact, this formula affords the individual at least two places to intervene; by changing either the perception of threat ("What's the worst that could happen if I don't make the cheerleading squad?") or shrinking the subjective value of the investment. ("Hey, it's only money, and we all know it comes and goes.") Once again, to change either of these is to change the very experience of anxiety.

You get the idea. An immediate change in your perception can bring about an immediate change in your feelings. How many times have you been frightened by noises in your house that you were certain were created by a blood-thirsty intruder only to learn it was the cat knocking over a lamp? In a split second the mind recalculates the situation—the dangerous becomes benign—and the symptoms of anxiety screech to an immediate halt. There never was a real danger or threat, but that didn't matter. You perceived a threat (intruder) to an investment (your life), and anxiety was the response; isn't this almost always the case with anxiety? Remember: anxiety is never reality, but it is created by your perception of reality. Dr. Richard Carlson, psychologist and author of *Don't Sweat the Small Stuff*, offers two basic rules to manage stress (anxiety): 1) Don't sweat the small stuff. 2) It's all small stuff.[3]

The Dummy Lights

Let me make an important point very early in this book. Anxiety, like all emotions/feelings, begins as our friend. Whether you believe in a divine order, evolution from primordial ooze, or a combination thereof, anxiety is designed to alert us to the potential dangers in our environment. The following comparison will illustrate this point. Your car's dashboard probably comes complete with an array of "dummy lights," indicating emerging problems with fuel, oil, tire pressure, windshield wiper fluid, and so on. These lights are so named presumably because smart people keep a careful watch over these important functions of their automobile. When your car's dummy light reads oil, for instance, you are alerted to the potential danger of your engine malfunctioning somewhere down the road. The message is this: dude, your car is low on oil; please respond appropriately.

So how do you respond? Do you ignore it and keep driving? Do you pull a hammer from the glove compartment and smash the light to pieces? Probably not, because you are smart enough to realize that the dummy light is your friend. It can help save your car's life, provided you respond appropriately.

Back to anxiety. Your body's dummy light is going on and conveying a message: Your investment is being threatened; please respond appropriately. Scott's dummy light was ignited by the threat of college expulsion. So what do you do when your anxiety light is illuminated? Do you ignore the message and keep going? Do you smash the dummy light by drinking alcohol or taking a tranquilizer? Or do you pay attention to the anxiety and figure out what the investment is in your life and what represents the threat?

This is the approach we'll take in the pages ahead: learn to understand your anxiety so you can respond most appropriately to your internal dummy light. For now, let's look at what happens in the brain to signal your anxiety dummy light.

Your Brain

Understanding the exact workings of the brain when processing anxiety—or any emotion—requires the specific and advanced training of a neuroscientist. Even then, there would still be questions that have to be answered. But this is a self-help book, so I want to make concepts simple, if not simplistic, and immediately user-friendly and helpful.

Let's borrow an explanation from the National Institute of Mental Health on how anxiety works in the brain. When you perceive a danger in your environment (the threat), there are two "sets of signals" immediately launched to different parts of the brain. The first set of signals conveys information to the cerebral cortex, the thinking part of the brain. Here the situation is analyzed and explained to the self as being dangerous, threatening, or even catastrophic.

The second set of signals takes a direct pathway to the amygdala, the emotional headquarters of the brain. Here the fear or anxiety response is triggered for instant action (fight or flight), often before the cerebral cortex understands what the exact threat is. For example, the amygdala ignites the stress or anxiety response at the first flashes of light in the rear-view mirror before the cerebral cortex can correctly interpret the lights as belonging to a tow truck and not a ticket-toting police officer.

The amygdala, in sending the signal for fight or flight to the nervous system, ignites the sympathetic nervous system, which induces the heart to increase the volume of blood pumped, diverting the blood away from the digestive and sexual/reproductive systems in favor of the major muscle groups to prepare to fight or flee. Likewise, stress hormones like adrenaline and cortisol are released in greater volumes to energize the body to combat the perceived threat. At the same time, this fear/anxiety/stress response becomes "etched" in the amygdala as a protective measure for future episodes. In other words, unless something in the brain changes, flashing lights in the rear-view mirror will become programmed to elicit anxiety (stress response) every time the brain perceives them. Hence, you are at war with your own brain (the original Civil War) when you attempt to reverse the pattern in which anxiety has become the usual response to life's everyday situations— driving, grocery shopping, dating, or playing competitive racquetball. How do we win this battle of the brain?

Joshua is a 14-year-old high school freshman with a rare gastrointestinal illness. The symptoms of his disorder are not so much abdominal pain, gas, or diarrhea. No, Josh's main bugaboo is a surprise attack of nausea that often culminates in projectile vomiting. As you might imagine, Joshua would prefer to be struck by lightning than "blow chunks" in front of his 14-year-old peers.

The issue that convinced Josh to get counseling was this: every school day he lived in utter dread that today might be the day when he spewed vomit like a green fountain of puke. Josh's imaginary scene was further catastrophized by the belief that this would make him the butt of jokes around the entire high school.

Emotions, including anxiety, are not the byproduct of reality, but of our perceptions. Nothing terrible had ever happened to Josh at school, but it didn't have to. As long as he imagined it, the scene was real and he was an anxious mess.

The opportunity to work with Josh prompted a long-since forgotten episode where I vomited scrambled eggs all over my second grade history workbook (I guess I preferred math) and everything/everyone else in my vicinity. I told this story not so much to gross out Josh as to make him smile, relate to his predicament, and, most importantly, reassure him that I survived the ordeal so well that I was now qualified to counsel other little pukers everywhere.

Further, I explained to him that anxiety was really about investment + threat; in fact, it meant there was an imminent danger somewhere. Really? Just where was the danger?

Well, Josh joined the high school band and disappeared from my regular caseload after only three visits, but he returned after a three-month hiatus. I inquired as to his health, grades, and, of course, anxiety. Josh shook his head and shrugged, explaining that he didn't worry about that anymore. It was no longer a problem.

"What happened?" I had to know.

"You know, what you said. 'Where's the danger?' There really isn't any."

I share Josh's story proudly with his permission and a special expression of appreciation to my second-grade teacher (whose name I forget) for not humiliating me.

We must learn that anxiety is a normal emotional experience, and our bodies are equipped to manage stress as a natural process. Often the media teaches us that we are not ever supposed to feel any discomfort. The moment our "dummy lights" turn on, we are told we can relieve our stress by turning to a pill, a drink, acting out, or other nonproductive means. Throughout this book, I will emphasize the importance of addressing anxiety rather than avoiding it by engaging in counterproductive behaviors. Stay with me as we explore "normal" anxiety.

ANXIETY BUSTER

Overwhelming or Manageable?

It is a rare person these days who comes to see a psychologist and isn't "overwhelmed" by something. It is this very perception that most often prompts someone to pick up the phone and initiate that first appointment.

Take 67-year-old Ruth, the mother of two healthy, high-functioning adult women. I met Ruth in the hospital where she had been referred for depression and anxiety, conditions she suffered in addition to her primary medical illnesses of pneumonia and chronic obstructive pulmonary disease (COPD). Between Ruth's terrible coughing spells, she revealed that she didn't know if she had the wherewithal to survive these illnesses and probably didn't deserve to anyway. Ruth was sick enough to require family support but well enough to consider that "maybe my girls wouldn't have the time or willingness to take care of me."

You see, Ruth's ex-husband, the father of both children, was a raging alcoholic in every sense of the term. He raged and he drank, and when he drank, he raged even more. Ruth knew that the girls, who had never been hit, suffered intensely with a form of secondary trauma from watching their dad scream at their mom. Only after he broke the socket below her left eye with his fist did Ruth finally leave him for good.

But in Ruth's mind the damage was already done. On her back now with nothing but time to contemplate her past and present, she figured her girls would offer little help to her. After all, she was guilty of exposing them to "a horrible childhood." What could she realistically expect of them now? And that's when Ruth revealed how overwhelmed she felt.

In my considerable experience with patients who are reportedly overwhelmed, we note one very important truth: Overwhelmed is a perception, not a fact. Our goal then is to help the person find a way to be manageable or simply "whelmed." If anxiety is manageable, the person can function; if overwhelmed, the person will implode.

Consider the following analogy: A man can comfortably carry around three boxes all day without a problem. One day his boss adds two extra boxes to his load. The man begins to tremble until at last he drops all of the boxes and the contents fly everywhere. If we can help this guy by removing only the top two boxes, he becomes functional again. A disaster is averted. He goes from overwhelmed to managing.

Back to Ruth. All she needed was someone to understand her plight (including the fear of her daughters' resentment and potential retaliation toward her) and offer her some sage direction. "Call your daughters one at a time and tell them what you've been harboring for so many years. Apologize for what you fear you did and didn't do. Let them know what you need."

Ruth chose to trust me. Perhaps she had nothing left to lose. Predictably, her daughters reassured her that not only did they not blame her, they considered her the reason they were doing so well as adults. It was her courage they sought to emulate. They were happy to help her now that she was the one in need.

The top boxes were removed; Ruth was no longer overwhelmed. In time with good medical care, she was able to heal from pneumonia and function once again.

What would it take to turn your overwhelmed to manageable?

Exercise 1: Perception vs. Reality

In the blank spaces, describe three situations in which you worried needlessly only to realize that the outcome was far from tragic. In retrospect, what was your greatest fear (rejection, physical pain, homelessness, social humiliation, disapproval)? Try to unmask the fear that presents most frequently in your life. Where might that fear have originated? How might you rethink it now so that it loses its power to create so much anxiety?

EXAMPLE 1

EXAMPLE 2

EXAMPLE 3

Exercise 2: Investment and Threat

Write your investments and threats in the last five episodes of anxiety that you can remember.

INVESTMENT	THREAT
1.	
2.	
3.	
4.	
5.	

Exercise 3
As explained in Chapter 1, if our anxiety lights fires, one of our options is to smash the dummy light, that is, do something to reduce the anxiety that has no long-term problem-solving value (drinking alcohol, smoking drugs or nicotine, snorting cocaine, punching walls, aggressing against objects or people, and so on). Now think of what you might be willing to do to challenge some of these self-destructive behaviors.

Exercise 4

Ask yourself how life-threatening the real events/situation was on a scale of 1 to 10, 1 representing not much, 10 representing extreme. Then ask yourself how you reacted in that situation on a scale of 1 to 10, 1 representing chilled, 10 representing extreme. Your goal is to work on decreasing your reaction and this will help you keep life in perspective.

SITUATION

How life-threatening was this situation?

How did I react?

Lesson learned

Exercise 4 (continued)
SITUATION
How life-threatening was this situation?
How did I react?
Lesson learned
SITUATION
How life-threatening was this situation?
How did I react?
Lesson learned

2 Normal Anxiety

Anxiety is normal and is experienced by every living organism, right down to the sea slug.

—Dr. Neil A. Rector, PhD, C.Psych., research scientist at the Sunnybrook Research Institute (SRI), director of the Mood and Anxiety Research and Treatment Program, and director of research in the Department of Psychiatry at the Sunnybrook Health Sciences Centre

What Dr. Neil Rector fails to relate in the above quote is that the typical sea slug is a very poor candidate for psychotherapy, due to a rather limited vocabulary; plus, most are uninsured.

Rick is a 55-year-old civil engineer with a remarkably stable 30-year career. But with the recent downturn in the local economy, the city manager elected to let Rick go along with his six-digit salary. A desperate Rick sought civil engineering positions throughout the state until he finally landed one. Although it paid 20 percent less than his previous job and included a two-hour drive from home, he was relieved to be working. He accepted the position and rented a small apartment for the weekdays, leaving his wife alone in the marital residence until his Friday night return. Every Monday morning he woke up, drove two hours back to work, and mentally prepared himself for yet another week without his wife. The pay cut, the fatigue, and the loneliness all contributed to a feverish hunt for work in the area near his home.

One day, Rick's wife, Norma, found an open civil engineering position in the immediate vicinity. Much to her delight, she shared the news with Rick that night and excitedly reported that the new position offered a salary that dwarfed that of his original city job. The additional money, she claimed, could help them clean up some of the recent debt they'd amassed with the new apartment.

But Rick never applied for the job. It wasn't that he'd fallen in love with the new job or a female coworker (as his wife feared). There was no secret longing to avoid his wife, nor a self-destructive tendency to embrace the lonely nights and long commutes. It was something far less sinister. Rick tried to pick up the phone; he intended to email his resume. Instead, he froze and distracted himself with computer games and other emails.

You see, the local position listed qualifications for leadership skills that Rick was certain he didn't possess, despite his wife's protests to the contrary. "This is the time," said Norma, "for you to step up to the plate and do something special for yourself, your career, and your marriage."

Rick never answered her and would not discuss the matter again until he sat in my office. "I was paralyzed," he told me. "What if the job was above me? What if I failed? What if they realized that I was in way over my head and fired me? I don't think I could take another dismissal from a job. I'm still licking my wounds after the last termination—and that one wasn't even my fault!"

Normal Anxiety

And so begins our discussion on normal anxiety. Was Rick's anxiety—the type that "paralyzes" the individual and contributes to a sabotage of one's career and marriage—normal?

Well, yes and no. If normal means common or typical, then the answer has to be yes. As I wrote in Chapter 4 of our not-yet-classic book, *Your Mind: An Owner's Manual for a Better Life*, we all have an internal saboteur that attempts to protect us from failure and rejection. And as noted in Chapter 1 of this book, when you sense a potential threat to your system, you become anxious. Anxiety warns you of the danger that you might fail, and avoidance is a very common response to the potential of failure or rejection. In that sense, Rick's behavior was very normal. But so is applying eye shadow while driving, drinking a 900-calorie latte after aerobics class, or even smoking cigarettes. If 20 percent of the adult population smoked cigarettes, it would be considered normal behavior. So maybe the better question to pose is: is it healthy? To ask if Rick's behavior is healthy conjures up a much different response. Self-sabotage, avoidance, paralysis, or however we want to label Rick's behavior is never healthy. So is anxiety ever healthy?

Healthy Anxiety

Anxiety is the neuropsychological response to the perception of threat to any investment. If the children in the street are playing too closely to your new Ford Focus and that situation makes you nervously look out the window every two minutes, you are experiencing anxiety. But how can that be healthy?

Responding appropriately to anxiety like the dummy light in Chapter 1 hopefully makes life a little better. If anxiety is used as an internal warning for potential threat prompting a corrective response, then anxiety is indeed healthy. For example, if you feel anxious whenever you see your wife flirting with your neighbor at parties, that anxiety may contribute to a healthy response of civilly discussing the issue with her. Keying your neighbor's Hyundai is considered less healthy. Not to mention illegal.

While anxiety becomes a problem and can be overwhelming if you obsess on negative thoughts, it can also serve as a catalyst to heighten awareness of personal goals, investments, or hopes. Let's explore other ways that anxiety is a friend with a helpful message rather than a self-destructive (and self-constructed) enemy.

Fear/anxiety (I use the terms interchangeably because there are no biochemical differences between the two) is necessary for the survival of any species. The deer survives as it does because it is fearful of other species, including humans, and outruns its enemies to safety whenever possible. Again, the investment is the deer's life/survival, the threat is the predator, and the anxiety alerts the deer to respond appropriately by running. To return to poor Rick, his deer-in-the-headlights response of paralysis would have spelled death for him in the animal kingdom. (Luckily, Norma has chosen not to kill him.) *In truth, anxiety survives because it helps species to survive.*

The latest research shows that people with Social Anxiety Disorder exhibit a poor connection between the amygdala and the frontal cortex of the brain. Unfortunately, these individuals with a reduced connection struggle to keep things in perspective. So instead of controlling their emotional reaction, their brains become overly excited. In these cases their brains react at full speed. Using behavioral therapy can help these individuals learn to gently apply the brakes.[1]

But humans have more to thank anxiety for than mere survival. Self-growth is also predicated upon anxiety. Show me a person with no anxiety whatsoever in his life, and I'll show you someone who is in an emotional coma. Without some threatening stimulus/stimuli in your life, you are not growing; you are functioning below the capacity of the previously mentioned sea slug. Your heart is beating, but your soul is dead.

Growth is the byproduct of successfully meeting a challenge. No challenge, no growth. Hence anxiety is necessary for growth. Unfortunately, the word *anxiety* has a negative indication. If you use a word with a more positive connotation such as arousal, stimulation, excitement, or charge to represent a challenging situation, you realize that the emotion of anxiety is predicated on your perception of reality, not the actual reality. What induces stress in one person is not automatically stressful for another.

Pat was a lovely woman in her mid-40s who had been content with her chosen sales career. But Pat's boss was not. He assigned her leadership of three new counties in her sales area in addition to the three for which she already had responsibility. Pat protested brilliantly, highlighting seven reasons why she could not handle the increase in responsibility. Her boss smiled as she spoke, congratulated her for her oratorical skills, and told her he had only one reason why she would be able to do it—he was the boss and he said so.

An angry, anxious Pat considered a retaliatory "I quit," but realized she would only be punishing herself. She decided to stay and absorb the extra workload. Within two months Pat was successfully supervising all six counties—to the tune of a 60 percent increase in commission, a renewed confidence in herself, and a bounce in her step. The lone drawback? She hated admitting that her boss had been right.

Pat's story is hardly unique. You may have been anxious when your Little League coach said, "Let's try you at pitching" or when your professor asked you to captain the debate team. Perhaps anxiety came when your mother asked you to babysit your younger brother or you decided to ask the secretary from the adjacent building on a date. For some of you, it was deciding to start your own business, agreeing to teach a class you'd not even taken in high school, presenting a new idea to the Board of Directors of your company, or assuming the challenge of becoming captain of your naked men's bowling team.

Judy was terribly anxious the week before her son and "very outspoken, hypercritical" daughter-in-law were arriving to stay at her home for nine days. Her fear was that she would be the recipient of the criticism that was almost certain to flow from the young woman's lips. So I made a simple suggestion to her: "When she arrives at your door step, smile big, throw your arms around her, and squeeze. Then tell her how great it is to see her."

Judy began her next session with "I've got some good news and some bad news. The good news is this: I hugged my daughter-in-law so hard that she instantaneously became *my best friend*! She's been gone three days now and I've already heard from her 11 times!"

"Wow! Great. So I'm asking, what could possibly be the bad news?"

"I don't want her as my best friend," she quipped.

Anxiety arrives when you hear of an upcoming exam, which prompts you to study. Anxiety appears when you learn that next week's opponent is ranked number one in the state and it elicits a response of hard work and preparation. Anxiety is spawned by learning that your quarterly taxes are due in two weeks and it inspires you to cancel a weekend shopping spree.

Anxiety reminds you that you are now officially out of your comfort zone. It is your brain's way of telling you that you are not finished growing, improving, learning, or developing. Anxiety is the body's way of convincing you that there is more to do—things to accomplish, goals to conquer, and dreams to realize. In fact, please accept my toast to the growth-seeking readers of this book: May you accomplish all of your childhood goals (including the one about becoming an astronaut). May you stare down and defeat the most menacing of bullies and take his lunch money. May you prove all of your naysayers wrong and live to hear them say so. May you earn more money than a Middle-Eastern prince and give it all away to cure cancer, MS, Parkinson's, and male pattern baldness. But may you *never* be anxiety free!

Yerkes-Dodson Study

In 1908 Robert Yerkes and John Dodson wrote a paper on arousal (not the erotic kind) and performance in which they described a law that suggests optimal performance occurs when anxiety is moderate. That is, when athletes, musicians, and other performers engage in their specific activity, they do their very best when moderately aroused (anxious). Neither the *absence* of anxiety nor the presence of extreme anxiety are good; moderate arousal (anxiety) is best. Let me explain.

If baseball player A experiences very little or no anxiety, it is likely that he is minimally invested in this particular game. Remember: it is investment plus threat that creates arousal/anxiety. (Maybe he's only making 12 million dollars this year, so he has little incentive.) With little investment, we can hardly expect him to perform at his best. He might not concentrate fully nor would he be inclined to "give it his all." Why would he, if he were not totally invested?

To the contrary, the same baseball player would not be able to do his very best if he were highly anxious. Why not? High anxiety tends to produce a "deer in the headlights" paralysis (much like Rick's behavior earlier in the chapter), which as you might discern is not conducive to hitting the ball out of the park or even remembering the words to "The Star Spangled Banner."

Remember, Yerkes/Dodson hypothesized this law in 1908. (To put this in perspective for our baseball analogy, that was the last time the Chicago Cubs won the World Series!) After more than a century of scrutiny, research continues to uphold their original theory. Moderate anxiety is good for performance. It's healthy, not pathological.

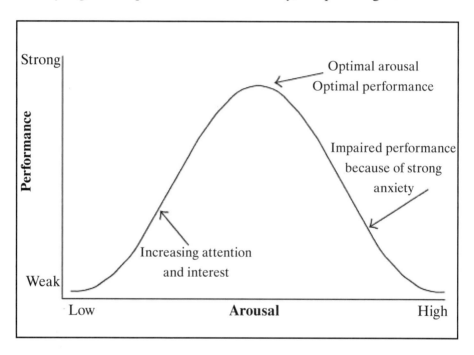

Let's explore the relationship between anxiety and performance from the perspective of a different type of athlete. David King, a two-time Olympic and eight-time British National pairs figure skater, relates the following from his personal experience: "You have to deal with anxiety head on, the worry you have will only increase if it is not dealt with quickly and efficiently. Again, you cannot ignore these feelings but embrace them and turn them into energy you can use in a performance or in everyday life."[2]

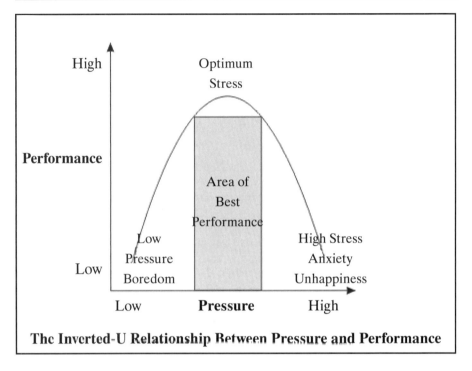

The Inverted-U Relationship Between Pressure and Performance

The hypothesis in the image is commonly referred to as an "inverted U." As you can see when an individual is bored, sleepy, disinterested, or unmotivated, his performance suffers. When the individual perceives too much pressure, he experiences the Law of Diminishing Returns. With too much cortisol or adrenaline, his heart races, his muscles tighten, he does not think clearly, and his behavior suffers mightily. Yet there is a point on this curvilinear arch where the system is awakened and alerted to the degree of optimal arousal and the highest level of performance. Arousal is natural to the system. It is healthy, adaptive coping that allows an individual to perform at optimal levels.

Frequency, Intensity, and Duration

So exactly when does normal or healthy anxiety progress to becoming a problem? When does it officially become an anxiety disorder?

To answer these questions, let me make an analogy. John goes into his physician's office complaining of a headache. Before offering any treatment, his doctor asks him three important questions:

1. How often do you experience headaches? (Frequency)
2. How much pain are you experiencing? (Intensity on a scale of 1 to 10)
3. How long do your headaches typically last? (Duration)

Now suppose John answers his doctor in the following manner: "I don't have many headaches—maybe three to four per year. On a scale of 1 to 10, I'd say my pain is a 5, and as far as duration, these puppies are usually all through in a half-hour or so."

That being the case, John's doctor might respond, "John, we all have headaches."

But suppose John had answered the questions a little differently: "I have these headaches three or four times a week. My head is splitting, Doc. It's at least an 8 or 9 on a 1 to 10 scale. They seem to last all afternoon, sometimes into the evening, always three hours or so."

Now John's doctor responds differently. "John, I think it's best to proceed directly to the emergency room!"

Normal, healthy anxiety is more like John's first set of answers—perhaps with a bit more frequency. Notice that normal/ healthy anxiety does not overtake or dominate a person's life. It is easily managed and subsides when the perception of acute threat is no longer present.

Dr. Cathy Frank, director of Outpatient Behavioral Health Services at Henry Ford Hospital describes pathological anxiety. "An anxiety disorder is different. Whereas normal anxiety is short-lived and doesn't usually interfere with your life drastically, Anxiety Disorder tends to be a chronic illness that has a significant impact on your daily function and may rob you of any joy in your life. Over 40 million people in the United States suffer from an anxiety disorder."[3]

Perhaps that's why anxiety disorders are often referred to as the common cold of mental illness.

So you get the investment + threat equation. But what type of situations most often contribute to creating anxiety in people? Can we predict where and when you are most likely to experience symptoms of anxiety? Funny you should ask, because in Chapter 3 we will tackle the topic of *common perceptual contributors* to anxiety.

But first, let me encourage you to invest your energies into the following growth-inducing exercises. Sure, they are challenging, but to quote Ralph Waldo Emerson, "Always do what you are afraid to do."

ANXIETY BUSTER
FOCUS = ENERGY

Psychologist Dr. Gary Emery coined a phrase that anxiety sufferers would do well to understand and remember:

FOCUS = ENERGY.

Essentially this means that where your attention goes your energy and emotions are sure to follow. Focus on your favorite comedy, and you are likely to smile and laugh. Ponder the antics of your ex-husband's attorney, and the feelings might change to anger and frustration.

Since we create anxiety by thinking thoughts of threat, sometimes all we need to do is to think about the same situation differently. For instance, "If I don't get the promotion, it won't be the end of the world."

Often we don't even have to rethink a situation to gain relief from anxiety. All we need to do is place our focus elsewhere. Allow me to illustrate. A woman with gephyrophobia (fear of crossing bridges) just returned from an exciting overseas vacation. Her husband picked her up at the airport and proceeded to drive over the most terrifying bridge in their area. But the phobic didn't panic.

She was so busy telling her husband about her amazing adventures in Europe that she paid no attention to the fact that they were facing her personal nemesis.

Her husband said nothing. Nothing, that is, until they were successfully across the bridge when he teased her by saying, "What happened, Chatterbox? You were so busy talking you forgot to hide under the seat!" The phobic realized that her husband was exactly right. By shifting her focus to the stories of her vacation, she was not thinking about the bridge in her customary catastrophic manner. In not thinking about it, she had no fear at all, and the ride over the bridge was as uneventful as the ride down her street into her driveway.

As a result, she realized that the phobia was completely arbitrary. It didn't exist unless she created it by thinking about the terrible things that could happen to her. If she put her mind elsewhere—singing, recalling conversations, creating shopping lists—she was not capable of panicking because she was distracted.

ANXIETY BUSTER

Your Anxiety Is Arbitrary and Not Based on Fact

When I was a child, almost all of the adults I knew wished they had a million dollars. They talked as if they knew that by attaining a "million clams" they would have everything they needed to be secure and happy.

Fast forward several decades. In the span of 48 hours, two patients—one male, one female—expressed feelings of overwhelming anxiety specific to financial ruin. But here's the rub: Both patients had a net worth of more than a million dollars! Both were approximately 70 years old and had never known what it was like to be without. With the downturn in the economy, both were obsessed with the possibility of complcte financial devastation. Ironically, both patients lived in homes that were totally paid off.

I reminded these individuals that they were in the top percentile of all the people in the world—wealthier than 99 out of every 100 people on planet Earth. Moreover, each was married to a strong, stable, loving partner.

But none of that information helped. Both of these worriers had experienced some recent losses and used those instances to view the future as a financial catastrophe waiting in the wings to destroy them.

Let this serve as a reminder of how arbitrary your anxiety is. Someone else would take your life circumstances and feel like the luckiest person alive.

Imagine switching lives with these millionaires. Would you be mildly concerned or perhaps elated by the change in circumstances? Would you, like them, be worried that your life was on the brink of financial disaster? Or perhaps you'd feel like you just won the lottery or, at least, feel safe and secure having just landed a million clams.

Exercise 1: Avoidance

One of the high school students with whom I work expressed his frustration with the waste of time involved in focusing on math. He claimed that because of his prospective major and career, he did not need to work on his math skills. Interestingly, he had always struggled with math. We discussed the possibility that he belittled arithmetic to avoid acknowledging his own difficulties with that subject. His sense of fear, apprehension, and angst regarding math compelled him to avoid it. Once he was willing to admit his anxiety about math, he shared a fantastic bit of insight. "If I try and I fail, then I'm the failure. If I don't try and I fail, I'm not a failure; I just didn't try." Fears associated with negative outcomes often lead to avoidance of the perceived anxiety-inducing experience, but with his new insight, this student was able to address his struggles and diminish his anxiety.

We tend to belittle areas where we feel insecure or inferior. Rather than face our fear of failure or embarrassment, we create barriers or talk ourselves out of doing the very thing that would be productive. Describe a situation in which you created a barrier or otherwise avoided doing something that you feared. Did you overcome your anxiety? How?

Exercise 2: Frequency, Intensity, and Duration

In Column 1, list situations that cause you to feel stressed or anxious. In Column 2, list the symptoms that you experience (headache, sweats, negative internal dialogue, panic). In Column 3, list how often the situation occurs. In Column 4, list how long the symptoms last. In Column 5, list on a scale of 1 to 10 (none to intense) the extremity of your symptoms.

For example, situation: public speaking; symptoms: hands get shaky, I feel like I could pass out, my mouth gets dry, I need to pee; frequency: every week at our sales meeting; duration: three or four hours, until the meeting after lunch; intensity: 8.

SITUATIONS	SYMPTOMS	FREQUENCY	DURATION	INTENSITY

Exercise 3: Situations

For each of the situations listed in Exercise 2, provide a list of the solutions you implemented to address your stress/anxiety. Which ones provided relief and which ones didn't help your symptoms?

Exercise 4

List situations in which you know other people become stressed or anxious, yet you do not. Write your thoughts as to how you perceive these situations in a non-threatening manner. What internal dialogue do you have about these situations?

For example: My girlfriend and spiders...she freaks out! It's just a spider, it can't hurt her!

Exercise 5

To end this chapter on a positive note and to help you see that even without wisdom and powerful resources you have learned to change your response to previous anxiety-inducing situations, write a list of situations that you would have previously reacted to with anxiety/stress. Write your thoughts about what has changed.

3 Perceptions That Contribute to Anxiety

Men are disturbed not by things but by the views which they take of them.

—Epictetus, AD 60

Bright lights, loud noises, the taste of rocky mountain oysters—there are but a few stimuli that are deemed to be universal stressors and consistently cause anxiety in humans. The rest are in your head.

For instance, let's look at the activity of skydiving. Some people panic over just the idea of skydiving, but others, rest assured, *choose* this activity every weekend to relax and get away from the stressors of daily life. Remember, it's all arbitrary. One man's source of distress and anxiety is another man's source of peace and solitude.

That said, are there any situations or predicaments that tend to contribute more to stress/anxiety than others? The American Psychological Association (APA) conducted an annual "Stress in America" survey to increase understanding as to what is creating mayhem in the hearts and minds of Americans. The stated goal would be to use the information to gain insight and help Americans decrease their anxieties.

In 2013, the top sources of stress included in the survey were as follows: money (69 percent of Americans); work (65 percent); the economy (61 percent); family responsibility (57 percent); relationships (56 percent); family health problems (52 percent); and personal health concerns (51 percent).

So let's look at three obvious sources of anxiety: fear of inadequate resources, fear of the unknown, and fear of rejection/disapproval, followed by 10 other situations that contribute to anxiety that you may not be aware of.

The Fear of Inadequate Resources (You are broke as S**T!)

That people are very worried about money and economic situations is hardly new. But recognize that money, labeled a "generalized reinforcer" by psychologists, represents different things to different people. To some, money means freedom to choose; to others, money equals success and a sense of feeling worthwhile. To many others, money represents security and peace of mind.

To perceive that there is not enough money can create anxiety for people in all three of the previously mentioned categories. In the first category, anxiety may come from the perception of entrapment: no money means no choices—you will stay at home and eat generic corn-flakes instead of brunch at the Ritz.

In the second category, the lack of money creates anxiety, because there is a perception of failure and inadequacy. Your uncle is a wall-street millionaire and somehow you ended up with a career of "in-between jobs." Your anxiety is the ever-present threat of feeling deeply ashamed and unworthy, especially around those you perceive as successful.

But the third category of people, you security seekers, are often plagued by anxiety that is created by catastrophic thoughts: you live in the fear that you will run over a nail, which will cause a flat tire, which will make you late for work, which will stoke your boss's ire, which will get you fired, which will destroy your only source of income, which will drive you to ask your parents for money again, which will set you up for a long lecture full of "I told you so's" and "you should come home and live in your old bedroom again," which will make you prefer to live under a bridge and push a grocery cart all day. Remember that your nervous system cannot distinguish between reality and imagination. Anything you think, believe, or ruminate on will make your body feel as if all your worst fears are coming to a theater near you.

The Fear of the Unknown

Another obvious source of distress and anxiety is the fear of the unknown. Put simply, this fear is all about the perception of vulnerability. Life is chock full of threats and dangerous situations, from a genetic predisposition to prostate cancer to the tragic realization that the posted photo of your daughter cuddling with your kitty yielded only nine likes on Facebook. But you never know what a new day has in store for you, as you only control a small percentage of the variables that impact your little world.

Take Virginia's story, for example. On July 1, 2005, her car was rear-ended on the way to work by a pre-occupied, non-breaking driver. Her car was totaled, and it took all the king's horses and all the king's men to put Virginia back together again. But she knew that doo-doo happens, and she recovered and returned to her regularly scheduled life.

That is, until July 1, 2012, exactly seven years later, when her car was rear-ended on the way to work by a preoccupied, non-breaking driver. Her car was totaled, and this time the king's entire staff was not enough to put Virginia back on the road again.

However, a little cognitive therapy and immersion in our book *Your Mind: An Owner's Manual for a Better Life* (another shameless plug), and Virginia was driving normally in rush hour traffic within two weeks.

On July 1, 2019, Virginia has very specific plans: she will stay at home, order pizza, and watch movies all day on the couch that backs up to the living room wall. Because you never know.

Rejection/Disapproval

In the many years of full-time private practice as a psychologist, I have seen scads of patients whose first appointment followed a failed suicide attempt. And although I don't have a statistic to quote, a very significant percentage had recently concluded that they were rejected, disapproved of, or inadequate in some manner. The perception that they were unworthy of being loved, accepted into the program, or not good enough to be included on the team/squad, is apparently so devastating to some that non-existence is a better option.

Hence, many people live in that fear of rejection/disapproval, coloring virtually all of their decisions from what to wear to with whom they mate. "What will people think of me?" is the question that looms behind all of the social phobias, including eating and drinking or even voiding in front of others. Most noticeably, it cripples people in their attempts at public speaking. Jerry Seinfeld famously noted that some people would prefer to be in the coffin rather than the person eulogizing the bereaved, because the fear of public speaking to them is greater than the fear of death.

> Did you know that when anxiety increases, academic achievement decreases both in male and females students? From all indications, anxiety has a greater impact on the academic performance of females than males. (Have your daughters read this book!)[1]

Disapproval and rejection is as consistent a contributor to anxiety as financial concerns or the unknown. The following is a Letterman-esque Top 10 list of anxiety-inducing situations that you already know, but may not know that you know.

1. The perception of powerlessness

There is a classic psychological study wherein workers were divided into two groups. The experimenters told the first group that significant noise would be made in the room on the other side of the wall that might be noxious to the workers. If at any point that noise was too much to handle, all the workers had to do was push a button on the wall and the noise would stop. (Of course, since the experiment was conducted by psychologists, the button on the wall wasn't attached to anything at all.)

A second group of workers was told nothing; however, they were exposed to the very same noises that the first group encountered.

The results of the experiment were most impressive: the first group of employees survived the noisy day at work with nary a problem. Their productivity was comparable to a typical day at work and, most significantly, they never needed to push the pseudo-button.

The second group, the one that was told nothing but endured the same noises, were not so successful. They made more errors in their work and complained of more stress-related symptoms such as headaches and gastrointestinal issues, and some employees even called off the remainder of the work day in favor of heading home to peace and quiet!

What happened here? Presumably, just the belief that we have some control (the button) over our environment is enough to promote tolerance and well-being. Powerlessness, on the other hand, tends to stimulate vulnerability and its natural byproduct, anxiety.

2. The perception of change

The second significant contributor to anxiety is change. There is an old joke that states, "The only thing that enjoys change is a wet baby." (Dr. Cortman's 2-year-old, Dylan, notwithstanding.) Nowhere is this point more colorfully illustrated than by the classic research of Holmes and Rahe back in the 1970s. The gentlemen devised what they called a Social Readjustment Scale, consisting of many items with a point scale of 1 to 100.[2] On their scale, changes are quantified and then tabulated for a 12-month period. For instance, the death of a spouse equaled 100 points, while a speeding ticket equaled only 11 points. According to their research, if a person scored more than 300 total points in a year's time, they had a 90-percent chance of a hospital admission the following year. The point, again, is clear: too many changes can overwhelm an individual and lead to physical and emotional breakdown.[3]

How do we explain the other 10 percent of people who seemingly endured numerous changes? Perhaps they are the same people who go skydiving to reduce stress.

3. The perception of insecurity

One of the more ubiquitous paradigms in all of education is Abraham Maslow's hierarchy of needs. His thesis is simple to comprehend: in order to achieve self-actualization—the highest state for humans to aspire toward—we need to satisfy a number of more primitive needs such as food, shelter, and reliable cable. Security, the belief that one is safe from all potential danger, is necessary to become self-actualized or realize one's full potential. The opposite, the belief that there is no safety or security, is a significant contributor to the creation of anxiety (the astute reader will remember that this is quite similar to the investment + threat formula). Just the perception that your job is in danger because of imminent layoffs, your pretty roommate is also attracted to the guy you'd like to date, or the sound of screeching brakes is coming from the car barreling toward you, can trigger significant surges in anxiety.

How important is the perception of security? Erik Erikson, the neo-Freudian icon who famously offered the eight stages of man, opined that achieving security through learning to trust is the single most important task that an infant can achieve in the first two years of life. Further, security is so important to humans that, according to research, the state of limbo—the inability to formulate a plan or ascertain a direction—is more difficult to contend with than even bad news!

✗ ✗ ✗

Ben and Rhonda were the envy of all of their friends. Their relationship seemed "perfect" because they enjoyed each other immensely and never seemed to conflict. But they had one insurmountable issue that kept them gridlocked in relationship limbo. Both were devoutly religious people, Ben was Jewish, and Rhonda was Christian. As such, they were incapable of agreeing as to how they would raise their future children. Consequently, they dated for 13 years, occasionally breaking up but always reconciling because they were convinced they were soul mates. They experienced relationship limbo because no solution could be reached between them. Finally, the couple was blessed with "bad" news. Ben was diagnosed with a debilitating case of multiple sclerosis (MS), which rendered him incapable of fathering children. The couple immediately got married and have enjoyed a very happy 20 years despite the fact that Ben is in a wheelchair and Rhonda is his primary caregiver.

As the research suggests, the bad news of the MS coupled with the sadness that there would be no children were considerably easier for the couple to assimilate than the perpetual state of limbo, wondering if they were ever going to resolve their seemingly insurmountable dilemma. As always, it should be noted that security doesn't really exist, it is only a state of mind, just like insecurity. There are stories of people living their lives with complete financial security because of a life insurance policy that they later learned was fraudulent. Others slept restfully in the knowledge that their spouses were completely faithful to them, only to learn posthumously from a secret journal that there were several marital indiscretions along the way.

> Something as simple as street lights are believed to speed up the "biological clocks" of songbirds. Songbirds exposed to light just 1/30th of that of a regular streetlamp made the birds breed earlier. Feel free to mention this research when telling your children about the Birds and the Bees.[4]

But your nervous system does not respond to the reality of your situations, only to your perceptions. If you believe you are insecure in your relationship, your job, your neighborhood, or the ice you are playing hockey upon, you will experience anxiety that parallels the degree of your investment (how important the situation is to you). Likewise, you may be living in complete peril living downwind from Chernobyl or next door to the Son of Sam, but if you aren't aware of it, there will be no insecurity and, therefore, no anxiety.

4. The perception of ambiguous roles (role ambiguity)

Jennifer is bright, intelligent, hard-working, and anxiety plagued. She works as a paralegal for a high-powered family law attorney in her town. Divorce battles, the bread and butter of their law firm, tend to yield a crop of highly vulnerable, anxious people who are spending a significant amount of their nest eggs to retain competent legal representation.

And therein lies the problem for Jennifer.

She watches helplessly as the money disappears from their retainers over frivolous expenditures like nonexistent phone calls and exaggerated meetings, consuming thousands of dollars from the clients. Jennifer is tormented, experiencing waves of anxiety in the wee hours of the morning and consuming Tums by the handful, because she feels trapped by the ambiguous demands of her position: 1) defend the integrity of her employer and 2) provide accurate, professional, and ethical services to their clients. Stated succinctly, Jennifer struggles with the dilemma of reporting her unethical boss to the authorities and quitting her job versus feeding/clothing her children.

Any time a person feels driven in conflicting situations (psychologists calls this role *ambiguity*) there is likely an accompanying anxiety.

But take heart, there's good news. Anxiety can be construed as a healthy agent for change (remember the dummy lights from Chapter 1?) and peace can replace the turmoil when a cognitive resolution is reached. Jennifer found a suitable solution to her dilemma: after close to two years of "inner nervousness and early morning tummy aches" Jennifer found another position in a smaller firm for slightly less money. She justified the financial regression by the realization that she would compensate for the lost wages with peace of mind and restful sleep, and with the savings she'd have from no longer purchasing Tums.

5. Vulnerability: the perception of losing your "blankie"

Dylan, my aforementioned 2-year-old, never travels far without his diaper bag, three or four spare diapers (you never know), wipes, snacks, water, a pacifier, and of course a blankie. Curiously, the blankie has his name on it, despite the fact that he cannot read. But it provides reassurance for him that is second in importance to only his parents.

Joan, although roughly 67 years older than Dylan, also has a blankie with her name on it. Of course, it is a figurative blankie, made of compulsive rituals rather than fabric. You see, as a little girl, Joan was molested repeatedly by family members, the very people who should have been protecting her. As such, she has lived her entire life experiencing considerable anxiety symptoms, especially claustrophobia (the fear of being trapped), as she was by her abusers, and hyper-vigilance (the need to constantly survey her environment for potential dangers). In other words, Joan cannot seem to relax because to do so would be tantamount to letting her guard down. Relaxation to abuse survivors like Joan is experienced as vulnerability. Think of a rabbit in an open field. Even on a beautiful, sunny afternoon with no predator in sight, there is always a need for alertness, nibbling food with eyes always scanning for the potential of a predator. One can only imagine that there are no moments of complete relaxation for the bunny (unless she gets therapy), as it might interfere with her very survival.

Joan, of course, is considerably more self-aware than the bunny, as she is in therapy and realizes that her anxiety, although designed for survival/self protection, is actually now *counterproductive* because it makes her miserably nervous in her own skin and compromises everything from travel in airplanes to simple elevator rides. Worse, unlike the bunny, there is no benefit to Joan's anxiety and avoidance behaviors, as her predators have been deceased for half a century and no one has abused her since she was 6 years old. But when asked to imagine how it would feel to release her anxiety and fear, Joan's honest answer was "more fear." The anxiety, ironically, has become Joan's self-protective blankie. And since no one has attempted to hurt her for so long, it feels as if her anxiety is working to protect her!

Is she hopelessly stuck in her anxiety? Gratefully, no. She, like Dylan, can learn to release her inner blankie by replacing it with other skills and tools as will be described in the subsequent chapters.

6. The Perception of needing perfection

Doc Miller was everybody's favorite physician. He was brilliant, had a great sense of humor, kind bed-side manner, and he did house calls long after everybody else in town had stopped. The only person in that little southern town who didn't want to emulate Doc Miller was his son, Bill. You see, even though the birth certificate read William Miller, everyone knew him as "Doc Miller's boy." So, the only way Bill figured he could carve out his own identity—his grandfather and paternal uncle were also physicians—was to do something, anything, other than medicine. Bill went into the military, far away, literally, from his dad and the perceived pressure of following in his father's considerable footsteps. The pressure to succeed followed Bill in his travels abroad, but he responded marvelously to the challenge, making his way up the ranks in short order. In Bill's mind, nothing short of Admiral—the very top—would suffice, because only that type of success would adequately compare to his father's remarkable achievements.

But an accident, a seemingly benign error in judgment, occurred on Bill's watch and literally sank his ambition to climb to the top of his branch of the service. Although Bill was not responsible for committing the error, he was in charge and, therefore, contributed to the perception that he was no longer qualified to wield that type of responsibility and leadership. For the record, Bill was no longer unblemished. And, unlike his father, he was not perfect.

Bill retired with full honors and appropriate accolades, a stellar career in the armed services. But he carried a persistent, nagging anxiety that he soothed with his clandestine relationship with Captain Jack Daniels. It was only after his wife threatened to leave him for the umpteenth time that I met Bill and learned about the anxiety that he carried in his life-long effort (and failure) to achieve perfection.

> Did you know that individuals with anxiety disorders are two to three times more likely to struggle with a substance use disorder during their lifetime as compared to the general population?[5]

Bill knew he had to put the bottle down for good, but, in and of itself, quitting drinking did not replace his anxiety with peace and contentment. Bill had to realize that his perfectionism was self-created in an effort to be adequate, good enough to be called "Doc Miller's boy." Even that insight was profitable, but not curative. He also needed to realize that his father was extremely proud of him, as were his wife, kids, friends, and all of the men he shepherded in his military career.

None of these people, I suggested to him, would have cared for him any differently had he acquired one more rank. It was *his* sense of inadequacy that prompted the pressure and anxiety, not theirs. But perhaps the clincher for Bill was a discovery he made in the midst of our work: by retiring early, he was able to spend the last three years of his father's life at the old man's bedside. Bill knew that his promotion would have spoiled that opportunity. In retrospect, the chance to provide regular house calls to Doc Miller was priceless and more important than an additional stripe on his sleeve.

7. The perception of imaginary threats being real

If anxiety is all about the perception of threat, then it is not necessary that the threat is real. When it comes to our nervous system, remember that perception trumps reality every time. Take Jeremy, a 4-year-old preschooler referred to me by the emergency room doctor. Jeremy had recently developed a phobia (irrational fear) of pooping. Thankfully, Jeremy wasn't grappling with this disorder for very long; his mother reassured me that he pooped gracefully and effortlessly up until three days ago.

The emergency room physician completed a series of x-rays, which revealed that Jeremy had no obstructions, so some fluids were administered to expedite the flow. However, after several more hours without productive output, the doc recommended that the little boy meet with a psychologist, as he believed the behavior was self-induced "withholding."

Upon examination, Jeremy was able to identify that there was a contributing cause to his self-induced constipation: it was only recently that he watched "Shark Week" on television. He related how scary the sharks were in the program. Jeremy pieced together that sharks swim in water and, in fact, his toilet also contained water. He admitted that he was terrified that one of these vicious man-eaters was going to "bite my butt when I'm pooping." I asked Jeremy how big these sharks were. He said 8 to 12 feet. I asked about their circumference by making my arms form a wide circle. I then inquired as to their exterior, whether they were hard or soft. Jeremy responded, "'Hard because they shot tags that bounced off." Finally I asked, "How big is the pipe on the bottom of your toilet that the poop goes down?" He made a circle with my thumbs and index fingers. With this knowledge, I took one of the cute stuffed animals that I have on my bookshelf, a soft seal, and asked Jeremy to push this soft toy through the circle shaped with my thumbs and index fingers. After unsuccessfully squishing the soft toy and trying his best to force it through the circular shape made by my fingers, he finally stopped and realized that his fear had no basis in reality. Immediately, upon this new awareness, he turned toward me and asked one simple question: "Can I go to the bathroom?"

Your particular story may lack the cute, innocent punch line, but don't we all carry imaginary threats? Chest tightness is construed as a fatal heart attack. Spousal tardiness becomes an extra-marital affair. Your womb, active with kicking last week, is quiet this week, which to you guarantees a miscarriage. Your boss's lack of response to your completed project could only mean that she hated your work and will be terminating your employment any day now.

Imaginary monsters lurk everywhere you are invested. To be anxious, all you need to do is to believe the monster exists. To borrow an anonymous quote, "Don't listen to everything you think."

8. The perception of unfinished business

The great Fritz Perls, father of the school of psychotherapy known as "Gestalt," was a pioneer in the theory that people need to complete their unfinished business to achieve peace. Stated another way, there will be no peace unless you finish the things in life that matter most to you.

Human beings seek closure. Think about it. Who makes half of their bed or mows 90 percent of their lawn? Are you ever satisfied with a partially finished manuscript or painting? A room you started to repaint? Unfinished items have the power to disrupt our equilibrium and disturb our peace. But how do we complete things that are impossible to finish?

Deborah, a widow in her late 40s, was referred to me by her primary care physician. She had lost her husband a little more than one year prior in a tragic, work-related accident. She had the usual symptoms of grief, including sadness, despair, loss of pleasure in the things that once mattered, and so on. But Deb was unusually anxious because of an inability to gain closure on her husband's untimely death. He was unloading a truck at his work site when he was struck by another truck traveling rapidly in reverse. Deb was beset with a significant, recurrent dream of this incident, waking with a flood of anxiety and one burning question: "Did my husband suffer before he died?" Her inability to answer this question prompted her to obsess on his final moments of life but never to reach any degree of satisfaction through her self-inquisition.

I was able to help Deb understand that if she wanted to move out of her self-imprisonment, she would have to find a way to release this question from her psyche, one way or another. She decided there was a way to gain more information; she could order the incident report at work and read the witness accounts and the coroner's report. There was just one problem: she didn't believe she had the courage to read the material. Still, she ordered the packet and brought it with her at her next session.

After the cursory hellos, Deb began the session by handing me the accident report, claiming that she would not read this on her own but trusted me to read this to her. When I reached the portion of the report describing the accident, I proceeded gingerly but honestly, reading verbatim that the truck hit her husband solidly and then ran him over with both tires on the driver's side of the truck. I heard a quick, but very audible, gulp emanating from Deborah, as she absorbed the witness's account.

She thanked me repeatedly and said that she had what she needed; she could allow herself to release the obsession and conclude once and for all that he had not suffered and, therefore, she no longer had to. I never saw her again. The unfinished business of his suffering was now finished and, hopefully, so was her recurrent anxiety.

9. The perception of being overwhelmed

Almost 100 percent of all people presenting with mental-health issues have one thing in common: they perceive their current life circumstances as overwhelming. That is, situations, relationships, and conflicts in your life have reached a place where you believe that you are no longer able to carry the burdens effectively. It is as if you can comfortably walk around life carrying three boxes. Suddenly, for one reason or another, life hands you a couple of extra boxes to lug around on top of the three you are already holding. Of course, instead of finding a way to drop a box or two off the top, you are on the brink of releasing all five of the boxes crashing to the floor, taking with it all of your efforts to remain a stable, in control person. You are overwhelmed!

Such was the case with Randall, the CEO of a successful manufacturing company. Randall was a big believer in the notion that no good deed goes unpunished. His deed was to make his small company a staggering success—a money-making machine in the three short years that he had been perched at the top of the pole. Based on that turnaround, his company was being purchased (or "devoured," as he called it) by a much bigger corporation that wanted to retain Randall, but make him a district manager. To keep his job, Randall had to learn "a new language," develop an array of new skills, and direct a core of "complete strangers." All of this, of course, from a new office in a new town. Randall's salary was almost doubled, but to hear his rendition of reality, he was regretful and resentful of the changes he encountered. Once again, he was overwhelmed.

Randall needed to understand that overwhelmed is a perception, not a reality. Some people are overwhelmed by the birth of one child; others comfortably parent children by the dozen. His perception that there was too much change and too much to learn is actually what caused his anxiety. His new bosses expressed confidence in Randall and formulated what seemed to be a realistic game plan for his new responsibilities. With a little self-exploration, he discovered that, at the bottom of his anxiety, he was overwhelmed and ultimately fearful that he would fail.

A little reality testing was in order. Randall had to be re-reminded that his company's excellence was due mainly to his innovativeness and leadership. The very reason for the merger was his success; it was not likely that he would suddenly become a "failure." Randall decided that the way to overcome his perception of his being overwhelmed was the same as the oft-quoted method to eat an elephant—one bite at a time.

Hence, he replaced his mantra of "I'm overwhelmed" with the statement that, "This is a lot but it is manageable and I will succeed." Finally, we created a new word. He was no longer "overwhelmed" but "whelmed." We defined that word as, "A lot, but manageable." Within three months he was promoted again with a brand-new opportunity to feel overwhelmed. This time, he handled the challenges without succumbing to disruptive anxiety.

10. The perception of entrapment
The only way out is through.

—Robert Frost

As you'll see in Chapter 7, the central ingredient in panic attacks is the perception of entrapment. The more acute the sense of being trapped (as if stuck in an elevator), the more you are inclined to panic. Less acute situations, a toxic relationship for instance, is more likely to produce generalized anxiety symptoms such as nervousness, insomnia, and irritability, rather than panic attacks.

Such was the case with David, a 42-year-old man who was chronically anxious and constantly miserable due to his perception that he was trapped in his work as a truck driver. A well-liked, hard-working employee, David had an unblemished work record with numerous promotions and accolades along the way. The problem, of course, was that he never wanted to work in that capacity; it was a job he "fell into" upon graduating from high school 27 years ago. David and his then girlfriend Sonya were the couple your parents warned you never to become: their first episode of unprotected sex culminated in an unexpected baby boy. Neither parent saw abortion as an option, so they decided to marry and become parents at the ripe old age of 18. College was no longer an option for David, but driving a truck for his baseball teammate's father was. And, even with the advent of two additional sons and what appeared to be a solid, stable marriage, David was trapped in his own private hell.

But, as always, perception trumps reality. Although David believed he was trapped, the reality was that he could retire with full benefits in just three more years. While that reality afforded David minimal comfort, he was less than inspired.

So, we examined what he'd be doing in a perfect world—one where he could work in any capacity he chose to. Interestingly, he stated he had always wanted to be a chef at a nice restaurant. He really enjoyed cooking at home and believed a job in which he could express his creativity in culinary creations would be delightful to him. So I asked David, "What if we used our time and resources to prepare for your retirement by looking into opportunities to attend a nearby culinary school?" With the money he had saved and the references he had amassed, he could likely accomplish his dreams, if he reinvested his energies in that direction. Of course, this redirection would require one thing: David would have to replace his perception of "I am a victimized, trapped man" with "hang in there a little longer and I can shoot for my dream of being a chef." At first, giving up the anxiety from his perceived entrapment was replaced by an anxiety of "Can I really do this?" Like the previously mentioned Randall, David also feared failure. But David decided that he owed his boys an example of a man who faced his fears and pursued his dreams.

Today he is the proud owner of a local downtown restaurant. Two of his boys work as busboys. Some days, when the lines and the hours are especially long, *they* feel trapped. But David is a free man.

Exercises
1. What causes me stress?
A. List the situations or relationships that cause you anxiety or fear.
B. List your perceptions that you have about the above situations or relationships.
C. List your feelings that you have about the above situations or relationships.

Exercises (continued)
2. If it's not perfect, it's not good enough.
A. List the situations in which you use all-or-none thinking.
B. Write the all-or-none comment that you think or say about the above situation.
C. Convert each all-or-none thought or feeling into a more realistic observation.

Exercises (continued)

3. I'm fine. You're nuts.

A. List situations that others perceive as anxiety-producing that you
   think are perfectly fine and that do not cause you any distress.

B. List the comments the others state that reveals their misperceptions.

C. What does it say about you that you can see these situations in a
   healthier light?

D. What can you learn about your perceptions after analyzing other's
   misperceptions?

4 Garden Tools

Positive thinking, visualization, and good
preparation are the main tools I used to be the best
I could be at a top event.

—David King,
Olympic figure skater

Beth is a successful registered nurse in a hospital's neonatal inten-
sive care unit (NICU), but couldn't understand why she was ordered to
drop everything (when she was knee-deep in newborn preemies) and
report to Human Resources (HR). "What couldn't possibly wait for the
end of my shift?" she asked herself. "Am I getting fired?" This catastrophic thought pummeled Beth into an immediate panic; by the time
she ventured across the hospital's massive complex to HR, she decided
to take an emergency Xanax in an attempt to quell her suddenly explosive anxiety. "What will I do if they fire me? How will I feed my kids?
I just bought that car! No one is hiring right now! What have I done?"

Upon entering the HR Department, Beth was handed a plastic cup
and ordered to produce a urine sample "STAT." Beth was not an abuser
of illegal drugs; she never drank before work. She was safe, she figured,
and relaxed immediately, easily yielding a urine sample for the nurse on
hand. But the meeting wasn't over. Beth was asked a series of questions
including, "Will we find any drugs in your system that have not been
prescribed for you by your doctor?" Beth was an honest person. She
couldn't lie. The emergency Xanax pill was not from her prescription.
It was her sister's. As such, she was breaking hospital policy by taking
drugs without a prescription. Gratefully, she was allowed to keep her
job if she willingly participated in outpatient counseling.

But I couldn't resist pointing out the obvious irony to her story. Beth was fine before the phone call from HR. She had no prescription because she had no anxiety disorder. Somewhere she heard from another nurse that carrying an emergency pill was a good idea if ever there was a crisis. But there was no crisis other than the one Beth created in her head by engaging in catastrophic thinking. By creating anxiety, she resorted to desperate measures that, instead of soothing her problem, almost cost her the job she could ill-afford to lose.

In this chapter, we will present simple garden tools that will work immediately to prevent, reduce, and even eliminate anxiety and panic, without the emergency pills.

Garden Tool #1: Understand Investment + Threat

Jim's Story

Dr. Shinitzky comes from a family of smart people, like his cousin Jim. Jim heard us lecture one day at a local bookstore on how anxiety emanates from the perception of threat to our investments. We continued to lecture about other somewhat interesting items, but Jim stopped tracking. He had a marvelous insight! A lifelong Chicago Cubs fan, Jim realized that he perpetuated his own anxiety and suffering—the Cubs last won a World Series in 1908—by maintaining his allegiance to them.

So, he made a very simple decision. It was now time to dump his "Lovable Losers" in favor of the nearby Milwaukee Brewers. The Brewers also never win the World Series, but that doesn't impact Jim. He doesn't care about them so his summertime blues have dissipated.

Kenneth is a well-to-do business guy in his early 70's. He is successful in life, except for the fact that his third wife threatened to walk if he didn't get his explosive anger under control. By his own admission, he's a great guy 95 percent of the time and an out-of-control ***-hole the rest of the time. It never happens with any other people in his life except his wife/wives. He was embarrassed, humbled, and frightened that he would strike out of marriage for the third time.

We needed two sessions to hit pay dirt: he wasn't out of control—he only "lost it" with his wife. Secondly, the only items that could upset/scare/arouse him were his investments. We quickly surmised there were two common denominators: money and power/control. If either of these issues were perceived to be threatened, he would go on the attack to defend his territory like a cornered badger. Of course, I explained, you can never win a fight with your spouse. It's like your left arm beating up your right arm. What did you win?

I suggested he change his thinking ASAP to reflect a more accurate reality: you have plenty of money; you will never run out, unless you buy the Yankees. Your wife is competent and responsible fiscally. She has never hurt you financially. She is your teammate and has your best interest in mind. There is no reason to yell at her—ever. Take a step back and always seek to understand her. The bottom line is this: You are invested in money, but there is no threat. You are invested in winning, but need to let go of that investment. You can only win if you both win. Use your energy to support her, tell her you trust and believe in her, and let go. That's how to win at marriage. Besides, divorce is quite a threat to your investments.

> Anxiety disorders (as well as substance abuse) often precede chronic low back pain. Interestingly, depression often appeared after the low back pain appeared. Caring for your mental health seems to be a vital way to protect yourself from chronic physical pain.[1]

Garden Tool #2: Focus = Energy, So Master Your Focus

Joyce was an 82-year-old woman with a history of significant anxiety issues, especially in social situations and tight spaces (claustrophobia), so she was delighted to hear that I would be speaking about anxiety at a local church facility. Anxious people often combat their symptoms by trying to manage their situation/environment. Joyce arrived a half hour early and sat right in the middle of the room with a direct view of the podium from which I'd be speaking. She was pleased to see that there was no one else there. No need to be anxious because, to Joyce, no crowds equals no threat.

Unfortunately for Joyce (but fortunately for me) little by little, the room filled up until there were no more empty seats and one poor man had to sit on the floor under the piano. By this time, Joyce was virtually stewing in her juices. She felt trapped, and the panic symptoms began to swell in her chest and abdomen. "I thought I would pass out, Doctor," she reported, "and then a funny thing happened. You began to speak, and I turned my attention to you and literally forgot all about my anxiety. It only occurred to me later, maybe halfway through the lecture, that I hadn't had a nervous feeling since you began speaking. It was like magic, Doctor."

Although I find pleasure in my patients believing I perform magical feats, there was no magic in what happened to Joyce. According to psychologist Dr. Gary Emery, there is a simple principle at work in operation Focus = Energy.[2] Joyce's focus was initially on the spacious, empty room, which provided no threat to her. When the crowd filed in, she shifted her focus to threatening thoughts like "I'm stuck now. I cannot leave the room without making a spectacle of myself and that would be horrible!"

But that focus shifted one more time to the podium, presumably thinking thoughts like, "Hmm, I didn't know that," "Boy, I can relate to that," and hopefully, "Wow, he is especially handsome."

Regardless of what Joyce really thought, her ability to distract her cognitions from a threatening collection of self-statements (I'm trapped) to something non-threatening (I can relate to this) *immediately* changed her feelings. Her anxiety was gone in seconds!

Let me provide one more example of how this works. Marsha was tragically victimized in a horrendous manner—abducted in a park at gunpoint by a total stranger. She was raped by this man and detained for several hours until she successfully staged a life-saving escape. Although she never saw the man again, the abductor continued to haunt her in so many aspects of her life (see Chapter 10 on PTSD). One such haunting was Marsha's inability to frequent a public park without experiencing terror and a feeling of doom and gloom. At the same time, Marsha was now a mother of two girls and vowed to never allow her trauma to ruin their childhoods. Hence, she would take them to the park and allow them to play while she suffered silently with flashbacks and extreme anxiety.

One day, she reported a very interesting development. She went to the beach with the girls and engaged in a Frisbee toss with the two of them for more than an hour. In so doing, she enjoyed her first peaceful afternoon in public since the abduction. How did she do it? She literally "forgot" about the incident because she had switched her focus from her horror to the Frisbee game and the delight of her girls. She was so caught up in what she was doing that she was temporarily oblivious to the people around her at the beach and not the least bit mindful of who looked creepy or potentially threatening. Although I saw this as a very positive outcome and a foundation to build upon, Marsha had a very different perspective. She engaged in self-chastising thinking, believing that by getting lost in the Frisbee toss, she was carelessly and unnecessarily exposing her daughters to potential danger. Since her guard was down, they could be in grave danger.

Nonetheless, she began to understand that her anxiety was actually a choice. She could focus on her horrible experience and employ the scanning, hypervigilent eye of a beach lifeguard or focus on spending time playing with her daughters. Put succinctly, she could live her life overprotecting them from potential dangers or participating in their lives. It was her choice, as wherever she placed her focus, her energy would certainly follow.

Researchers have found that the thicker the nerve-fiber bundle connecting the amygdala and the frontal cortex, the lower the levels of anxiety; if the connecting nerve-fiber bundle is not as thick, the more anxious the respondent.[3]

Garden Tool #3: Make a Plan

Here is a little secret: anxiety breeds in the tepid waters of chaos. That is, whenever there is disorganization, carelessness, and/or the lack of structure, expect a high level of anxiety. Why? Anxiety is about the perception of threat, and chaos is very threatening because the potential of danger is greatest when we have no semblance of control over our lives. (Recall Chapter 3 and the noisy workplace experiment.)

Kathleen had managed to gain more than 60 pounds after her 50th birthday. Always a very lovely woman who easily attracted men, her weight gain convinced her that she was no longer a worthwhile person. In fact, she was now so ashamed of her appearance, she was afraid to venture out, for fear that people would look at her critically. Most impressively, she had no idea what to do about her social anxiety, so she remained in the miserable sanctuary of her bedroom and devoured cookies, chips, and ice cream in an effort to provide self-comfort.

Without a plan, Kathleen was rapidly spiraling downward in a clinical depression, in addition to her anxiety. She needed a little direction and a great deal of encouragement. We put together a simple plan, one that included an exercise program, an endocrinologist, and a support group in addition to our weekly therapy sessions. With the advent of our plan, the anxiety plummeted significantly and immediately.

So why don't people take more control of their lives by making lists, structuring their days, and making plans? For one, making plans is time-consuming. But for another, to make a plan is also to make an investment, and once invested we are now vulnerable to disappointment and failure. If no plan is made, no plan is foiled. Hence, there needs to be the awareness and flexibility that almost all plans need to be revised along the way as the unforeseen developments in life are encountered. Keep in mind that flexibility is as important to mental health as it is in physical health. In other words, to reduce anxiety, make a plan and then plan on changing your plan.

Garden Tool #4: Learn the Serenity Prayer

We all know the Serenity Prayer. It's likely magnetized to your refrigerator, glued to your bumper sticker, and/or permanently etched in the hardware of your hippocampus (your brain's memory center). I've often considered this prayer as "mental health in a nutshell." Whatever you can't change, fix, or control, you need to release because it is out of your control and therefore isn't yours anyway.

But very often, life isn't as simple as having two distinct black or white categories. In fact, most challenges in life are a combination of making changes and accepting the inevitable.

For instance, most people refrain from rain dance rituals or prayers to the "sun god" because we tend to believe that the weather is not something we can control, fix, or change. There is a famous quote that states, "Everyone is always talking about the weather, but nobody does anything about it." But it's not as if there is nothing we can do about the weather. We can respond appropriately to today's weather report by donning a jacket, bringing an umbrella, staying indoors, postponing outdoor plans—whatever is most sensible. Dealing well with the weather includes understanding that it's not mine to control, but it's completely mine to respond to.

And doesn't almost every stimulus or situation you face warrant a combination of letting go and responding appropriately? You probably don't control the traffic, but you can decide what time to leave for the airport. You most certainly don't control the stock market, but you get to decide where to invest your money; and, just in case there is any doubt, you do not control your children's behavior although you can teach, discipline, nag, provide boundaries, lecture, issue endless guilt trips, and so on. You can't control; you can respond.

All relationships share that same common denominator of lack of control over others, while controlling only your response. One of the oldest recorded stories is found in the third chapter of the book of Genesis in the Old Testament of the Bible. According to the story, God informs Adam and Eve of their freedoms and limitations in the Garden of Eden. They are cautioned against eating the "forbidden fruit." And as we all know, the first couple famously disobeyed God's orders (much like your children), putting God in a position of needing to respond. According to the story, God responds by levying consequences but never by blaming Self (a potential lesson for all parents).

Perhaps he knew the Serenity Prayer and granted Himself the serenity to accept His powerlessness over His children and the courage to respond with consequences. Perhaps that's why we never read of God's weekly visits with his shrink.

> Listening to music reduces your body's stress level and strengthens your immune system, proving to be more effective in lowering anxiety levels than prescription drugs for patients about to enter surgery. "Listening to and playing music increases the body's production of the antibody immunoglobulin A and natural killer cells—the cells that attack invading viruses and boost the immune system's effectiveness Music also reduces the levels of the stress hormone cortisol." It has not yet been determined if the researchers dared to include death metal, gangsta rap, or Justin Beiber in the study.[4]

Garden Tool #5: Master Your Relationship Tools: Communication and Boundaries

Okay, so you get that anxiety is born of threats to things that matter to you. And you know that your family and loved ones matter, so naturally you can deduce that relationships contribute to a significant percentage of your anxiety. And now you understand that you don't control your loved ones, you merely respond to them appropriately.

So it's time to introduce two very important skills (tools) to help you respond well in all of your relationships: communication and boundaries.

Let me begin by issuing a challenge to you for *all relationships from now on*: communicate excellently. Be clear, concise, and to the point. Whether it's your spouse, child, mailman, or concubine, communicate as if your relationship depends on it. Often, it does. Leave no blanks for others to fill in inaccurately. Make it difficult for people to misinterpret you; express your feelings in the first person. Where appropriate, always be clear as to how important/loved/appreciated the person is that you are talking to.

Secondly, set impeccable boundaries. Let people in your life know that while you cannot control them, you can and will control your response to their behavior. For instance, "I will call the police if you hit me again." Or, "All papers received after the due date will be subject to a one letter reduction in grade." How about, "I won't sleep in a bed with a snorer?" Or even, "I won't belong to a group that would include me as a member."[5] For a more comprehensive discussion, check out the *Book of Boundaries* by John Townsend.

Anxiety, as aforementioned, is often a byproduct of chaos, unclear boundaries, poor communication, the perception of limbo, and/or the lack of control. Let me be clear: when things are not clear, you are more likely to suffer anxiety. The enemy of anxiety is clarity and organization.

Garden Tool #6: Act Like the Healthiest Person in the World

You are hopefully now well aware of the importance of flexibility in reducing anxiety. I'd also like to make a case for problem-solving. Nothing fancy, just good old-fashioned brainstorming to resolve the outstanding issues in your life. Sometimes there are no easy solutions to clearing up long-standing problems. Many times the only solution is to be flexible with those aspects of life that are simply unsolvable.

Let me illustrate what attitude, to me, encapsulates healthy thinking. Neil Simon's play, "Brighton Beach Memoirs," features a Jewish-American family, the Jerome's, living in Brooklyn circa 1937. As we all know, Adolf Hitler was amidst his reign of terror in Europe at that time. The Jerome's received a telegram from nervous family living in Europe looking to escape to the United States before it was too late for them. After reading the telegram, Mrs. Jerome looked about their tiny home and asked her husband in an anxious voice, "Where will we put them?" Her husband responded as if he were the healthiest person in the world (that is, someone who adapts appropriately to the changes and challenges in his or her environment, no matter the source) and said only, "We'll do whatever we have to do."

That's it. Nothing more. Why would I recall that line more than 20 years after seeing the play on Broadway? Because Mr. Jerome responded with what the healthiest person in the world would say and do. He couldn't very well write back and say, "We have too small a house. Sorry about your luck!" No, they should come, all of them, however they can get here. We will figure it out. I don't know the healthiest person in the world, but I am sure that the response would be positive, encouraging, realistic, and problem-solving.

I also know that my patients, when told that I have just injected them with the healthiest person in the world, become more rational, more logical, and less overwhelmed by their anxiety. They seem to discover a reservoir of healthy problem-solving cognitions, and are able to tap into that supply in short order. Interestingly, moments earlier, they were bereft of healthy responses, mainly because of viewing themselves as incapable and overwhelmed. When injected with "the healthiest person in the world," they are amazed by their transformation to someone who just might be up to the challenge after all. Why? Because besides the ability to locate problem-solving skills, the suddenly healthy one also stumbles upon the confidence that accompanies rational thinking. And confidence, I'm sure you know, reduces the perception of threat and, therefore, the experience of anxiety.

Garden Tool #7: Name Your Fears (Anticipatory Guidance)

So what is the difference between anxiety and fear? Theoretically, it's simple: anxiety is usually when your upset is about something vague and in the future, while fear connotes a more intense feeling that is specific and in the present. To me, the words and experiences are interchangeable.

So the next tool involves the skill of taking the vague dread of anxiety and turning it into a number of specific concerns. Let me illustrate. Roger is a middle-aged professional who was minding his business one evening but still managed to witness a violent crime. As if that weren't traumatic enough, poor Roger was informed that he would need to testify as to what he saw in court. The very thought of sitting on the witness stand was enough to send Roger into a panic and into my office.

One of the methods I used with Roger was to require him to specifically say aloud everything he was fearful/anxious about. As you might imagine, his fears centered around being made a fool of on the witness stand by a great white shark clad in an attorney's suit. So I walked Roger, however painfully, step-by-step through the events and behaviors of his future date when testifying in court. My rap sounded something like this: "You'll wake up that morning and go pee. You've done that before, right? And then you'll brush your teeth. You've got that down, yes? You can dress yourself, true?"

And so we went step-by-step: driving, parking, walking up the courtroom steps, raising his right hand, and listening to the bailiff's instructions. And then the big stuff. "You'll be asked questions by both attorneys. You've answered questions truthfully before, correct? And they may ask you some you don't know or don't remember, so what do you say?"

"I don't know or I don't remember."

"Yes! That's it. That's all you have to do. No study. No performance. No presentation. Just answer their questions truthfully and you are good." I was using a behavioral technique known as Anticipatory Guidance. This technique allows you to anticipate what may happen in any given situation and then prepare as to how you will respond. For example, "If I see my ex at the opera with his new girlfriend, I will smile, wave, and wish them well after.

Does snapping a rubber band on your wrist help you to stop a train of negative thoughts? According to the research, not so much. In fact, this oft-prescribed therapy technique may actually cause the opposite to occur if you attempt to suppress your thoughts. They may return more frequently and powerfully. What to do? Allow the thought and then walk it to the door of your mind and release it. If/when it returns, do the same again.[6]

Roger was relieved—and a little embarrassed—by the realization that he was a basket case over what appeared to be simple activities that he does ritually and competently in his daily life. At one point he even smiled and admitted "I answer more difficult questions than that every day—I'm a married man!"

But how does it help to name your fears specifically? According to research the mere expression of your feelings reduces the subjective distress.[7] Certainly the realization that your fears are benign and toothless further reduces your subjective distress. And that, of course, is a fancy way of saying: When you realize your problems aren't real, you can let go of your anxiety.

Garden Tool #8: Exercise

Unless you are exercising regularly, you are probably tired of hearing about it (when you should be exhausted from doing it). Forgive me, but you are going to read about it again. Why? Because I can't think of anything in the world that is so universally accepted as exercise. You can debate the merits of consuming milk, believing in God, even using sunscreen, but nobody debates the importance of exercise.

If you printed one piece of paper for each study that demonstrated the benefits of exercise for something or other—longevity, digestion, cardiac functioning, weight management, sleep, treating depression, diabetes, chronic pain, and so on—you could fill an entire gymnasium with paper. (I just made that last part up because it sounded impressive, but you get the point.)

Oh, and by the way, reducing anxiety is also on that list. According to mayoclinic.com, exercise decreases anxiety by releasing "feelgood brain chemicals" including neurotransmitters and endorphins.[8] Exercise also seems to reduce immune system chemicals that can worsen depression and anxiety and increase your body temperature, which can have calming effects. It has been said that exercise literally forces you to relax.

Of course, there are numerous psychological benefits as well. Meeting goals and challenges, losing weight, and getting in great shape all serve to increase confidence and self-esteem, which, of course, serve to reduce anxiety. Further, exercise can promote a better social life by connecting you with other recovering couch potatoes, which also promotes well-being and decreases anxiety. Finally, exercise is a fantastic coping skill because it works immediately to reduce stress and anxiety symptoms.

What to do? First, always check with your doctor. When you get the green light, the recommendation is very simple. Do whatever you are most likely to keep doing. Walking is easiest because it requires only that you have both feet on the ground, but swimming, jogging, lifting weights, Pilates, skiing, juggling relationships, and basketball, are also good.

Now here is something you will never read again in this entire book: put the paperback down now and go for a walk! I will be here when you return.

Garden Tool #9: Overcome Worry With Faith

*Worry is like a rocking chair: It gives you something to do
but gets you nowhere.*

—Erma Bombeck

As I discussed in Chapter 3 of *Your Mind: An Owner's Manual For a Better Life*, worry is a mindset/behavior that people engage in because there is a payoff. That may come as a surprise to you because rationally you know that worrisome thinking creates anxiety and distress and doesn't allow you to accomplish anything positive.

But as the Erma Bombeck quote depicts, worry does provide you with something to do and *keeps you attached to the issue* at hand. Releasing worry, as we saw in Joan's story in Chapter 3, contributes to feeling vulnerable. That is, worry feels like a protective shield.

But there's a second benefit to the activity of worry: it works. No, not really. It only feels like it does. Let's include another quote on worry: "Some of the worst things in my life never happened." We can all relate to worrying about horrible outcomes that never happen. And, according to psychologists, two things that occur together are associated. It's called the Law of Association. So if you worry about a positive read on your prostate cancer screening and the results are negative, you are rewarded for worrying. Your worry is now associated with the desired results of a cancer-free outcome. And psychologists will also remind you of this: behavior that leads to a positive outcome will likely be repeated. Stated simply, you worry and nothing bad happens. It feels as if it was your worry that warded off the negative outcome. So you worry again and again and continue to believe that you are actually contributing to the desired results. Soon, you worry about virtually everything.

> A two-semester long study of college students found that meditation practice significantly decreased their levels of stress. The study also found a significant reduction in their anxiety levels as well as their perfectionistic thinking. We suggest you teach children to relax and meditate before they even master toilet training.[9]

But worry does not work. In reality, it raises your blood pressure, increases your cortisol level[10] (the stress hormone that contributes to, among other things, the scourge of belly fat), and creates long unhappy days and sleepless nights. And, with apologies to our moms, it drives your kids crazy.

But what can you do to release worry? Again, psychologists will tell you never to take anything away from a person without replacing it with something else. (This is why after a painful breakup, a Maltese puppy can be helpful.)

So we aim to replace your worry with faith. Faith in what, you ask? Faith in anything that helps you to release your worry. Here are four types:

1. **Faith in God** or whatever you call your Supreme Being. People of the Judeo/Christian faith, for instance, have a myriad of promises from Old and New Testament scriptures that essentially say that your worry is useless, so trust God, who has the love and power to protect the birds and

lilies, supply all your needs, forgive all your sins, make your crooked ways straight, heal your physical ailments, afford you eternal life, and so on.[11] Think of an Allstate commercial. You are in the giant, protective hands of the living God who loves you more than you love your kids. So what is there to worry about? Research demonstrates that people of faith have an easier time facing death, have more joy, recover faster from illnesses. The lone exception is people who see God as angry and punitive.

2. **Faith in fate.** People who believe in fate say things like "It'll all work out." Or "Things always happen for a reason." Or even "What comes around goes around." They believe that since they don't do things to hurt others, in the end it'll be okay. But is that accurate? It doesn't matter. The fact that it is believed is all that matters to reduce/eliminate anxiety. Likewise, even if the previously mentioned people of faith are wrong about the existence of God, the belief still helped them assuage their anxiety.

3. **Faith in others.** I must admit I have no knowledge/skills regarding aviation, but I fly easily and comfortably. I do so mainly because I trust the knowledge/skills of my commercial pilot and the crew in the air and on the ground. I wouldn't know what to do to land the jumbo jet if it were in peril, but I believe the people in the cockpit do. Ironically, I arrive just as safely as the person sitting next to me who has worried him- or herself from New York to Florida. The only difference is that we attribute our safe voyage and landing to different causes: me to pilot competence, my neighbor to her worry.

4. **Faith in Self.** There are people who never spend an ounce of energy on worry because they believe that they are intelligent and competent enough to handle whatever life tosses at them. Some insist that if seven billion other people are surviving to a greater or lesser extent, they can, too.

Let me provide an illustration of how faith in Self tends to work. I ask a friend if he would be willing to do me a favor. I have a package that needs to be delivered today to 14th Street in Palmetto (a small town about 30 minutes from me that no one seems to ever visit). I tell my friend it's so important to me that I will pay him $100 for his trouble. He agrees. Then it occurs to me to ask, "Have you ever been to 14th Street in Palmetto?" He says, "No." I wonder what makes him so sure he can deliver my package successfully, if he has never been to the desired destination. He states simply, "I have been driving since I was 16. I know how to drive on American roads. I can follow directions. I even have GPS in my car. I know how to navigate the road ahead of me."

In order to release worry, you have to have faith in something or someone, even if it's you.

Garden Tool #10: Dwell in the "FOG" (Forgiveness, Optimism, and Gratitude)

There was a time not too long ago when psychologists seemed to study only unhappy or mentally ill people. Then came a movement, led by Martin Seligman and others, where it became fashionable to study happy/well people and find out what makes them tick. So now, after 30 years or so of "positive psychology," we have an abundance of research on how happy people think and what they do to steer clear of anxiety and depression.

Forgiveness

> *Unless someone like you cares a whole awful lot, nothing is*
> *going to get better. It's not.*

>   —Dr. Seuss

Let's begin with forgiveness. Healthy and happy people tend to forgive (let go) everything. They release all resentments, regrets, and carry no traces of bitterness. How does that matter? Resentful people tend to die younger than their non-resentful counterparts. They also are more prone to increasing their cortisol levels, suffer cardiac issues, strokes, clinical depression and yes, even anxiety disorders. Hanging on to resentment maintains the stress response instead of allowing the individual to return to a normal state of composure and equilibrium. Remember that peace, the polar opposite of anxiety, is the result of acceptance, of letting go. Resentment, bitterness, and regrets will always produce turmoil and anxiety, never peace.

So make sure you absorb this one important message: Letting go is not contingent upon what someone did to you. Whatever you may be carrying from mild disappointment to murderous rage, you will never find peace until you work through your pain and let go of your resentment.

Optimism

You know those annoying people who are always saying things like, "It's all good," "Everything happens for a reason," and "'Things work out in the end"? Well, it turns out they are on to something. Optimistic people live longer, are consistently happier, recover more quickly from illness, and yes, you guessed it, suffer from less anxiety. When I first learned of this, I changed my tune as a father: I now tell my 6-year-old, Melina, "You are an excellent listener over 10 percent of the time."

It's really quite easy to understand: when you believe things will work out in the future you are not focused on potential threats. And, as well as you know your own name by now, it is the perception of threat that creates anxiety. Not the belief that everything will be okay. Or that all will be forgiven. Or that he or she never meant to hurt you, or that your Dad is in heaven. Those optimistic beliefs may be nothing more than wishful thinking without any factual basis, but it doesn't matter. Believing them "makes them so" (as William Shakespeare noted hundreds of years ago). At least as far as your nervous system goes.

What's more, you can learn to think optimistically. Even if you have never coughed up a positive thought in your life, you can learn to do so now. Check out Martin Seligman's book, *Learned Optimism*. You'll love it. I'm positive.

Gratitude

Fran is 67 years old and has never had a date in her life. It's not that she hasn't wanted to, it's that no one has ever asked her. You see, Fran was born with some facial deformities rendering an unsightly appearance. She was teased and bullied as a child and has survived countless surgeries on her eyes to correct her vision. In sum, her life has not been easy, and from every indication, she has been quite lonely.

But to hear Fran tell it, you'd think God was always smiling on her. Her gratitude for what she does have is compelling: she is grateful for her job, her health, her good parents, her recovery from a drinking problem, her dashingly handsome psychologist, you name it.

And gratitude, like forgiveness and optimism, has an abundance of research to validate its importance: grateful people are happier, live longer, make more money, have lower blood pressure, and, of course, have less anxiety. Their focus is on how blessed they are now, not how frightening their future appears. Besides, if God has shined His favor on them all their lives, why would He stop now?

Garden Tool #11: Eliminate All Conflict

Way back during the Roaring Twenties, in 1924, an American writer named Max Ehrmann wrote his classic poem entitled "Desiderata" (The Desired Things). The treatise began with a borrowed quote from the Apostle Paul's letter to the Romans, "As much as possible, without surrender, be on good terms with all people." Sounds a tad unrealistic, I'm sure, to be at peace with everyone from your mother-in-law to your daughter's boyfriend with the nipple piercings.

But it's true. We now know that conflict, the polar opposite of peace and tranquility, is harmful to the body, not just the soul. Emergency room professionals relate that very serious and even fatal myocardial infarctions (heart attacks) follow heated verbal arguments at home. Likewise war veterans have significantly more physiological and psychological issues when exposed to combat. Even children of divorce are significantly more likely to suffer emotional problems and psychiatric illnesses when exposed to ongoing conflict between their parents. In fact, conflict between parents is the single greatest predictor of pathology in children of divorce.

All of this is basically saying that conflict is bad for your heart, mind, and soul. And needless to say, conflict fuels anxiety because it excites the nervous system and induces the stress response just like any other perceived threat. The opposite of conflict, of course, is peace, which is also the opposite of anxiety. And how do we get to peace, you ask? Acceptance.

Once again, everything you cannot change, fix, or control must be approached with a healthy, sober attitude of acceptance.

Is there ever a time for conflict? Of course. Historically speaking, without conflict, there would be no peace. But most conflicts are not worth waging. From the perceived slight to the texting driver who swerves into your lane, it rarely pays to enter a skirmish. Choose your battles wisely; to everything else, let go and accept.

Garden Tool #12: Be Like Spiderman

Superheroes, in case you haven't been watching, are quite prevalent in our society. They appear in comics, TV, and big screen adventures on a regular basis. From Batman to Superman, we are inundated with epoch battles between good and evil.

But almost all superheroes have one thing in common (besides a marvelous wardrobe guy)—they all live a normal life as a civilian: whether we are talking about shoeshine boy (Underdog), Dick Grayson (Robin), or Peter Parker (Spiderman), they all have the ability to leave their superhero triumphs and challenges in the box with their hoods, masks, and fantastic tights. That is, they conduct their work and family responsibilities until it is time to don their colors and their crime-fighting mojo.

So should you.

If you want to champion your anxiety, it is wise to leave your personal issues in the parking lot and assume your superhero status the moment you walk into your domain as a nurse, personal trainer, or youth pastor. To wit, I don't want my brain surgeon reviewing his morning squabble with his partner when he's carving into my corpus callosum. Likewise, my defense attorney would not be doing me justice if she were worrying about her foreclosure instead of my protection.

The superhero known as you owes your employer, clients, and family the same discipline of shedding your work issues with your uniform. Likewise, your personal issues do not belong at work. Your boss pays you to focus on work challenges, not domestic ones. It is highly unprofessional to contaminate your professional duties with personal worries.

Think about your coworkers: Do you admire the woman who complains non-stop about her lazy husband while underperforming at work? And how annoyed do you get when your coworker spends his work time anxiously climbing the walls? (Unless he *is* Spiderman.)

Taking control of your focus (see Tool #2) will better help you increase your productivity and manage your anxiety.

Garden Tool #13: Locate Your Options

As you will see in Chapter 6, most panic attacks are born out of the perception of entrapment (or perceiving the self as overwhelmed). And, to review, perceiving or believing that you are trapped is all that matters in triggering a message to your amygdala to hit the anxiety/panic button (see Chapter 1). Remember, reality is inconsequential; your nervous system follows your perceptions, not the facts.

So let's talk about entrapment, the perception of being stuck or trapped. Unless you are a prisoner of war, you are probably not trapped. The great Victor Frankl, a well-known survivor of a Nazi concentration camp once wrote, "Everything can be taken from a man but one thing: the last of the human freedoms—to choose one's attitude in any set of circumstances, to choose one's own way."[12]

Your "entrapment" is predicated upon a choice you have made and are continuing to make. You can leave your job, relationship, or mindset if you needed to. Sure, there would be discomfort and/or sacrifices to be made but let's face it, there is virtually always a way out, if not more than one.

I'd like to have a dollar for every story I've heard of someone going through with their wedding day, in spite of the realization that the impending nuptials were a huge mistake. Why? Because down payments were made, invitations were sent, and people were flying in from Cheboygan. But were they really trapped or was it more about avoiding embarrassment and humiliation? Sure, a down payment would disappear, but needless to say, that pales in comparison to a divorce attorney's retainer. The truth is, there is rarely an insurmountable trap.

Randi tells me that she is learning to master this tool of finding options. She has one of those husbands who frequently gets upset at other drivers because all of those "a-holes" don't seem to drive as well as he does. He yells, swears, and threatens to arrange a meeting with their maker before the scheduled day. For years, Randi was a victim of his adult temper tantrums, absorbing the venom that was intended for those other bleepity bleeps, like second-hand smoke.

Until recently, that is. Randi learned that she didn't have to ride with her husband; she was a big girl and she could drive her own car. But her husband hated that she was driving to the very same destination—especially with gas at four bucks a gallon—so he promised to clean up his act. The only time he regressed was when Randi had her knee replaced and was temporarily dependent upon him again. But Randi rose to the occasion once again and figured a different method to find an escape option. Preferring to get lost in the beat of the music, rather than the sound of the ranting and raving, she began humming the music to her favorite old album and disappeared from his bad behavior.

This was excellent preparation for what was next: Randi's first vacation in two years was stalled when the pilot announced that there would be a "slight delay" before take-off because of "mechanical issues." That ever-so-slight delay lasted for just over eight hours, culminating in a range of human responses (from the other passengers) from yelling and screaming to napping and snoring. But Randi, my patient who always perceived entrapment, was now prepared to find options. Her mindset included thoughts like, "I'm okay, and we'll get going eventually. I have options: I can read, sleep, talk, or even catch up on emails." She even surprised herself with employing grateful thoughts including: 'Thank God I'm on vacation, I have the time. It's great that there is food and drink and two nice people next to me to talk to—I'll be fine."

Remarkably, eight hours on a stalled airplane and no panic attacks. Why? Because Randi found lots of options.

Garden Tool #14: Breathe!

You probably don't know how to breathe. I know, you've been doing it just fine since your first breath. But if you are prone to anxiety or especially panic, you may need to learn to improve the one behavior you thought you had mastered from the beginning.

Most people don't pay attention to their breathing. You may be one such person. You have other important things to worry about. Maybe you learn to pay attention to your breath when you were learning to swim or play a wind instrument in school. Those are places where the regulation of your breathing is obviously important. It is always best to avoid inhaling when under water.

As discussed earlier, when you are in fight-or-flight mode, your breath quickens to quick shallow breaths, known as hyperventilation. When you breathe this way, you tend to use your shoulders to move the air in and out of your lungs. Although this may work well enough in the short term, it can feed into the cycle of symptoms that create—or are perceived as—anxiety. Using your shoulders in this manner increases tension. Muscle tension may result from anxiety and may also trigger your brain to prepare for a threat. Also, this way of over breathing makes your blood levels of carbon dioxide low and low levels of CO_2 sends signals to your body to breathe even more. Of course, to continue breathing that way simply feeds the problem. Hence, a vicious circle ensues. In fact, breathing like this makes you feel like you are going to faint or pass out, causing symptoms that include dizziness, light-headedness, weakness, shortness of breath, a sense of unsteadiness, muscle spasms in your hands and feet, and a tingling feelings around your mouth and fingertips.

Rather than breathing shallowly—or by using the top parts of your body like your chest and shoulders—breathing from your diaphragm (no, not the contraceptive device, that would be awkward) will result in achieving an appropriate and healthy level of oxygen in your bloodstream. Your diaphragm is a muscle that separates your chest from your abdomen. You may picture it as a muscle that is at the bottom of your ribs. Its job is pretty basic: when it contracts, it tightens. When that happens, it seems to pull your lungs down and opens your airway, causing air to flow into your lungs. When the diaphragm relaxes, or lets go, the downward pressure is released and the air in your lungs is naturally exhaled. This, in turn, prevents or counteracts symptoms such as shoulder tension, dizziness, and shortness of breath. This is important because these symptoms not only are physical expressions of anxiety but they are also signals to your brain. Again, something is terribly wrong and you need to prepare. A threat is imminent!

Diaphragmatic breathing is also referred to similar names like belly breathing, abdominal breathing, and deep breathing. You may have been advised to take a deep breath through your nose for a certain count and then exhale for a similar count. Sure, that's a start, but to be good at deep breathing, it requires practice.

Learning to deep breathe may still feel silly or awkward. Many people have spent a lifetime holding bellies in, so it may take a while to become accustomed to breathing in such a way that the belly protrudes or sticks out. Here is how to learn to become a belly breather:

Diaphragmatic Breathing Practice

1. Find a quiet place where you can practice and lie down on your back on a flat surface. You may find putting a pillow or rolled up towel behind your knees makes this position more comfortable. Do so it if helps.

2. Place one hand on your upper chest and the other on your belly. Between your ribs and your belly button is a good place to start.

3. Close your eyes and take a slow breath through your nose and expand your belly as your breathe in.

4. You will notice that the hand on your chest will barely move at all while the hand on your belly will rise quite a bit.

5. Pause as you normally would when you breathe and then tighten your stomach muscles and slowly exhale, allowing the air to gently escape through your mouth.

6. You will now notice that the hand on your chest has still barely moved while the hand on your stomach has fallen.

7. Pause naturally and then repeat steps 3 through 6.

8. Practice this exercise until you are comfortable and it feels natural to breathe in this way. You may want to use a ruler (from sternum toward your belly button) or a book placed where your hand was when you were first doing this. Practicing these items can help you see, as well as feel, the results of this practice.

9. Pay attention to the rhythm and flow of your breath. Try to make it as effortless and smooth as possible.

10. Once you are comfortable and confident in your practice of diaphragmatic breathing, you will move your practice from the floor to a comfortable seated position.

11. Practicing your breathing while sitting will likely feel odd at first but will become easier—just as it did on the floor—with patience and practice.

Garden Tool #15: Clean up Your S*** Off the Floor!

At some point in your life, not doubt, you've moved your home or office. With every move comes the relocation of stuff. Lots of stuff. You do your best to situate all of your old stuff into the new place. But, invariably, there's leftover stuff with no clear destination. And what happens to this stuff? It ends up on the floor, waiting and waiting to find its final resting place. You trip over the stuff, it becomes an eye sore, and it is just plain in the way. But you still don't know what to do with it.

Relationships are kinda like that, with unresolved issues sitting on the floor of your partnership, robbing you of a joyful connection and contributing to unnecessary anxiety. Take Shawn and Denise, a married couple of 14 years still struggling with the same intimacy issues that dominated their honeymoon year. Consistent with the age-old stereotype, Shawn would like to be intimate two to three times per week; Denise would be all set with the schedule of a full moon—once a month is fine. Not a shockingly unique problem, but one that remains a source of distress and anxiety, for both partners. Shawn avoids bringing up the topic of sex, fearing rejection, and then resents Denise for his anxiety and hurt feelings. Denise avoids responding to Shawn's affection, for feat that all affection is merely a precursor to intercourse. Naturally, this contributes to Shawn feeling rejected, hurt, and back into an angry withdrawal from Denise. And so it goes, a vicious circle that has no immediate solution in mind. Both parties feel (correctly) victimized by the other one. And who wants to be intimate when you resent your spouse so deeply?

My recommendation for the couple is the same bit of advice offered to the movers: get your stuff off the floor and put it somewhere. Anywhere. Agree to something. Be intimate once a week on a regular day. Be affectionate and warm every day. Engage in bonus intimacy whenever possible. Work something out. But in any case, seek to resolve age-old issues. Put them away. For every item removed from the floor contains a promise of resolution, hope, and a reduction in anxiety.

Garden Tool #16: Be the Master of Your "A Words"

For those of you who have ever been called an "A-Word," take heart. It is time to learn to be the master of your A-words. Anxiety is, of course, an A word. But you knew that. To master your anxiety, here are some other A-words that it will be necessary to champion:

We can begin with avoidance, the Darth Vader of A-words when it comes to anxiety. All human behavior is purposeful and goal-oriented and meets a particular need, or it simply would not be repeated. And that includes avoidance. How does avoidance make it into your behavioral arsenal? As you know by now, whenever you are facing a situation that is linked with thoughts of threat or perceived danger, there are feelings and symptoms of anxiety. But if you can manage to figure out a way to avoid an encounter with your nemesis (your calculus exam, rush hour traffic, cross-country flight, and so on), you will feel great relief. Your anxiety will be significantly diminished, and you will do your happy dance.

For those of you who took psychology 101, the removal of uncomfortable, noxious, or painful stimuli is called negative reinforcement. The dilautid that relieves your kidney stone, the pacifier that quiets the screaming baby, the influenza that attacks your teacher on the day of your final presentation—these are all negative reinforcers. So negative reinforcers are, in fact, a positive thing for you, because you experience relief. And, back to psych 101, relief, like anything that is perceived as pleasant, will likely be repeated. So you are more likely to avoid rather than confront the anxiety-inducing situation the next time. Hence, a vicious circle is established: You experience anxiety at the thought of confronting an important situation/person/project → you avoid getting around to that confrontation and experience great relief as a result → your anxiety increases at the prospects of facing it the next time → you avoid again.

Delores joined a Bible club at her house of worship, a group of nine or 10 ladies who decided that they would take turns hosting the Thursday evening get-togethers at each person's home. It only took two Thursday evenings for Delores to conclude that she was well out of her league. The first two women lived in palatial homes—far nicer than Delores's humble abode. Delores was scheduled to host week 4 and talked herself into feeling sick several days before her turn. She called the woman from week 9 and asked if they could switch turns. Her plan worked and Delores felt significant relief from her avoidance. But a couple of weeks later the anxiety returned as she imagined the ladies walking into her home and wincing at the meager square footage, low ceilings, and modest furnishings. Just that thought produced a skyrocketing anxiety level within Delores, interfering with her productivity at work and her capacity to sleep.

Delores pushed the avoidance button one more time by telling an unbiblical lie to the group that she had to help her husband with his new business on Thursday nights and would need to drop out of the Bible study group. (And soon afterward, the church.) Although this was a lame, see-through excuse, it still provided significant and immediate relief to Delores. Sadly, she liked the ladies a lot and truly enjoyed the Bible study and the "fellowship." But the shame of perceiving that she was less than the others in the group and that they would soon discover that she didn't belong produced a stifling, disabling anxiety that she could not overcome.

Or could she?

Actually, Delores had choices of other A words besides avoidance. Let's begin with words like *admission* that there was a discrepancy between the socioeconomic status of most of the other ladies in the group and Delores. She could not only *admit* to that, but she owed it to herself to *accept* that reality and respond *appropriately*. What response would have been more appropriate?

Delores would have done well to *approach* or *address* her issue directly in order to relieve her anxiety. For instance, to state to the group one Thursday evening something like, "I'm enjoying the Bible studies thoroughly and your company immensely and I need to thank you for this opportunity, but I must admit after being in several of your houses, I feel intimidated at the prospects of having you in my home. It is neat and clean, but so much smaller than all of yours. I'd love to have you and you are most welcomed to join me in my home on the 27th."

Any similar expression by Delores would likely engender warmth and comforting responses by the other ladies, who would probably thank her for her candor and appreciate her courage and humility. The anxiety would be permanently replaced with a sense of satisfaction with herself and pride for staring down her sense of inadequacy. Also, expressing emotions openly in a group often increases closeness and intimacy with the other members', a significant upgrade over dropping out of church in a lonely, defeated state of shame.

As you will see in the second half of this book, there is no anxiety disorder that will improve as a result of avoiding what one is afraid of. All anxiety disorders must be acknowledged, accepted, addressed, and approached head-on to champion the battle with your foe.

Master your "A words." Then do your happy dance.

Garden Tool #17: Talk Back to Yourself

We've all caught people talking to themselves. Admit it, you've laughed and labeled them "crazy" for conversing with no one in particular. Turns out, they may be more sane than you know.

According to psychologists, especially those with a cognitive bent, we should all be talking back to ourselves—out loud—when we struggle with symptoms of anxiety. So what do you say to your anxious inner Howard or Ruth? How about something like this: "Look, Howard, it's me, your Outer Self. Please don't think I'm creepy, but I've been watching you. Now I know you need to prepare for your presentation to the investors. Let's practice it until you know it like the Pledge of Allegiance and then share it with your dad in a mock interview for some helpful feedback. Once you've mastered your presentation, you can deliver it to the investors to the best of your ability. At that point, it's in the hands of (God, Jehovah, Allah, Fate, the Universe, nothing—you pick). I want you to know that you have worked very hard on launching this new venture and I'm proud of you."

You will have done all you can do at that point. So let it go. If they love it, great. If not, you learn what you can from the experience and move on. Remember, not everything works out the way you'd like it to. Don't let anything defeat you. You are a champion just doing your best. Now go "break a leg."

Why talk like this to Self? Because it works! Your nervous system believes every word you say to Self. And again, your beliefs trump reality when it comes to influencing your nervous system. To think thoughts that conjure up threat is to create anxiety. To re-think your situations with thoughts that promote confidence, well-being, or manageable outcomes will decrease/eliminate anxiety. And you know what is better than thinking calming thoughts? Saying them out loud. Making them audible words will establish them as solid foundations of the way that you think, feel, and are.

So, how crazy is that?

Garden Tool #18: Do Like They Do In Brooklyn

The 60's pop band known as The Brooklyn Bridge had a hit single called "The Worst That Could Happen." Little did they know at the time, their song title would become a therapeutic technique for psychologists everywhere. In fact, the whole technique is nothing more than asking the question, "What's the worst that could happen?" From your vague worries to your specific fears if you are anxiety prone, it's an important question to answer.

Evelyn is an educated, highly cultured woman in her early 80s. She maintains a tremendous respect for her doctors and treating professionals. So when she was beset with a significantly negative post-surgical outcome—one that her surgeon reassured her could not happen—she didn't know how to deal with her situation. So Evelyn stewed quietly in her own juices, growing more upset and defeated with each passing day. She wanted to express her sense of violation to the surgeon directly, but that was not how she was raised.

Evelyn's primary care physician became concerned that she was slipping into a depressive funk so she referred her to me for a consultation. Despite her efforts to conceal them, Evelyn's frustration and resentment were easily detectable from the first mention of her botched surgical procedure. Her feelings, it appeared, were certainly commensurate with what happened, especially when considering how her surgeon dismissed her concerns. For Evelyn to recover from her funk, we concluded that she needed to express her frustration and hurt directly to her surgeon. But that was something she was ill-prepared to do. I might as well have asked her to complete an Iron Man triathlon. She couldn't possibly confront a doctor. And not just a doctor, but a...surgeon.

So that's when I had to pop the question: "What is the worst that could happen, Miss Evelyn?" She hemmed and hawed and finally shrugged. "What's he gonna do, reverse your surgery? Call your parents? Ground you to your room?"

Evelyn wrote a careful, but expressive letter, detailing her post-surgical pain and suffering and her sense of betrayal by her surgeon. She brought the letter to the surgeon and respectfully read it to him. So what was the worst that happened?

The surgeon apologized—sort of—and stated that he had never had that outcome before and would be inclined to tell his future patients about the potential of it happening to them. He, in fact, was a better doctor because of Evelyn's courage to share her feelings.

She, in turn, moved out of her emotional funk, which, given all the variables, was the best that could happen.

Garden Tool #19: Perform Feats of Magic

Frank is a magician. I only knew this because he was able to make his chronic worry over finances disappear in one shot. To be fair, it was our sixth session when Frank emerged as a magician.

A 68-year-old man with a significant history of anxiety and marital dysfunction (a lonely wife who complained about Frank's inability to communicate with her), Frank would repeatedly sit for hours and worry about what he would do if they ran out of money. You see, Frank's dad had financial issues and was prone to being unhappy and anxious about all things related to money. But in my humble opinion, Frank sensed that he had enough money to not have to worry. Besides he has a financial manager. Most people who are about to run out of money do not have a financial manager. I asked Frank what Louis, his financial manager, thought about his financial predicament. He was told that he was in good enough shape to travel and have some fun. He then told me that Louis had been his financial manager for 30 years and have never steered him wrong.

"Don't you trust Louis?" I inquired. "Of course I do. He's the best," Frank answered. I then asked Frank if he did this on airline flights—spent the entire time fretting and worrying or if he were inclined to trust the pilots and their navigational skills. He claimed that flying (and trusting) was no problem. He always flew in complete comfort.

It occurred to Frank where I was going, if he could trust and let go in one area of life, he possessed the necessary skill set to generalize this to other areas of life. So that day he made a conscious decision to start trusting Louis and stop worrying about his finances. And, according to Frank and his wife, he has never worried about money since that day.

This is a true story except for one small part. Frank is not really a magician. He's a regular guy who decided to stop worrying and enjoy his life.

Garden Tool #20: Knowing About the Unknown

A major source of anxiety for human beings is thinking about facing situations with unknown components—starting college in a faraway state with all new people, for instance. Even though every situation of every day contains aspects of the unknown, it is still much easier to take the same drive to the same office building to do the same job you've done for 17 years, then a new job in a new place.

Sheeba had accomplished much in a short stint in treatment, including ending a 30-year painful marriage. She decided that even bigger life changes were necessary, so a move overseas to Europe to resume a career in international finance was now in order for her. Sheeba believed that this was certainly the right decision; she would be returning to her home with friends and relatives that she missed terribly. But so much had changed in the many years that she had lived in the States that it seemed to Sheeba that she was "returning home to a place she'd never been before." And so, she experienced a noticeable spike in her anxiety level, especially in the hour of the morning before the alarm. Why the surge in anxiety? What was the perceived threat? Sheeba said it was all about "facing the unknown." There is an old saying that people prefer the devil they've known to the devil they don't, even if it's an evil one, because familiar is easier.

But Sheeba was an avid meditator, spending anywhere from one to two hours each morning engaged in meditative rituals. My clinical recommendation seemed quite logical to me—combine her meditation with strategic positive self-talk, including the following: "I'm returning to the country I love by choice. My favorite people live there. I will survive all facets of my life. I can travel wherever I'd like. Most significantly, I'm taking me with me and leaving my love-less marriage behind me for good. I will never allow myself to be trapped. I am free, happy, and excited to begin this new phase of my life!"

Immediately after implementing this new exercise, Sheeba noted that the free-floating anxiety related to the unknown had been replaced with excitement, hope, and a sense of "I can't wait to go!"

Garden Tool #21: Slaying Your Dragons

Dragons come in various shapes and sizes, and yet are all-powerful until confronted and slain. Seventeen-year-old Jordan had never been on a date in his young life. While that in and of itself is not unusual, this seemed like a significant problem for him because he wanted to go to the prom, badly. There was a girl, one he "liked a lot, but why would she go to prom with me?" he asked. You see, sometimes dragons take the form of 17-year-old girls.

Leigh was not any girl. She was intelligent, lovely, and the varsity shortstop for the softball team. That was intimidating for Jordan, who had never reached first base with any girl before. Anxiety, specifically due to fear of rejection and failure, was Jordan's challenge and the reason his parents sent him to me for treatment.

Our job was to slay dragons together, and we only had two weeks left before the prom. I informed Jordan that running from dragons (avoiding) only made them appear bigger and scarier the next time. We needed to approach the dragon and muster up the courage to ask Leigh to the prom. But how?

He decided to surprise Leigh at her next home ball game to cheer her on and make his move. Jordan was armed with more equipment than the catcher, carrying a banner, a softball, and a dozen roses. As far as Jordan was concerned he had one chance to score, so he dug in the batter's box and swung for the fences.

The banner read, "Go Leigh! #12" on one side, but the flip side was flashed right at Leigh when she left the infield at the end of the game. It merely said: "Prom?"

Jordan then tossed her the softball containing a question, "Will you go to the prom with me?" And, just in case the banner and softball were insufficient, the roses were self-explanatory and a big hit with Leigh, not to mention her teammates.

As far as Leigh was concerned, Jordan hit one out of the ballpark. The prom date was official and, most importantly, Jordan's self-esteem waxed while his anxiety waned, completing a double-header sweep over the fiery dragons.

5 Power Tools

You have brains in your head.
You have feet in your shoes.
You can steer yourself any direction you choose.

—Dr. Seuss

You're learning to master the garden tools I taught you in Chapter 4. Fantastic. With a little practice, you can reduce you anxiety levels significantly. But for some of you, it'll take even more than those garden-variety hoes and shovels.

What is your best tool?

Janice, like everyone else, has her anxious moments, especially as a vice president of a local bank. She knew that her anxiety was more in the driver's seat of her life than she was, so she scheduled an appointment. I asked her what tools she employed to aid in her struggles with stress and anxiety.

"Tools?"

"You know, like a hammer, wrench, or power drill makes it easier to complete projects at home. What tools do you employ to help you cope with these work challenges?"

Think about what tools you possess in order to conquer anxiety successfully. Try to have a variety of garden and power tools in your toolbox, so you'll be prepared no matter what situation comes your way.

For those of you with true anxiety disorders—diagnoses we will explore in the next five chapters—it may require supplementing your coping saw with a "rotozip," your Phillip's head with a screw gun, your hammer with a mechanical forging hammer.

I want to share some power tools for anxiety and anxiety disorders, tools to use in construction with a trained, licensed psychologist or psychotherapist in professional treatment.

Although I will introduce the power tools to you here, please apply them, at least initially, under the supervision of a trained professional. (I relish the opportunity to say, "Don't try this at home, this is for trained professionals!")

Power Tool #1: Psychotherapy
Somehow our devils are never quite what we expect when we meet them face to face.

—Nelson DeMille

When the companies that sold oranges and orange juice wanted to sell more products, they created a clever new slogan that convinced us of the following: "Orange juice. It's not just for breakfast anymore."

It's time to borrow that mindset, if only for an illustration. Psychotherapy. It's not just for the mentally ill anymore. In fact, according to the abundance of research that now exists, psychotherapy is helpful for virtually anything that ails you. Where do I begin?

If your marriage is crumbling to pieces, psychotherapy can help glue it back together again. If you are grappling with insomnia, psychotherapy can help you replace your "whys"? with Zzz's. If you are still stuck in resentment after being bullied, rejected, neglected, betrayed, beaten, molested, teased, dominated, used, overlooked, subjugated, ignored, belittled, underestimated, swindled, raped, discounted, cheated on, stolen from, spied on, stalked, cyber-bullied, flashed, abducted, mugged, or tortured, psychotherapy can usually help. In fact, from back pain to weight gain, from problems going out (agoraphobia) to problems coming out (acceptance of homosexuality), psychotherapy is the treatment of choice. As you will see in the chapters that follow, there *is no better* treatment option for generalized anxiety, panic disorder, agoraphobia, phobias, post traumatic stress disorder, social anxiety, or adjustment disorder with anxiety features than psychotherapy.

So, how does it work? Psychotherapy begins with human connection. Research confirms that caring, supportive, and validating human connection provides the very framework for healing. Also, as you will read in the chapter on PTSD, the *expression* and *release* of emotion is curative. In fact, psychotherapy changes the biochemistry of the brain. How? Evidently by releasing painful emotions and altering cognitions (thoughts, attitudes, and beliefs) the effect is analogous to placing a different frame on the same old picture of life—the world looks different.

With good psychotherapy, it becomes possible to say goodbye to a deceased loved one, a horrible childhood, or a narcissistic lover. Likewise, you can say hello to a life without panic attacks, compulsive rituals, or nagging self-doubt. You can learn to muster the courage to speak in public, fly in an airplane, or ask out the goddess in your chemistry lab.

But when it comes to treating anxiety disorders, the most successful and "evidence-based" schools of psychotherapy are cognitive/behavioral (changing the way you think and behave) and mindfulness based (learning to relax and focus in the here and now). I will attempt to introduce you to some of these treatments and techniques in the pages ahead.

Collectively, the authors of this book have facilitated in the neighborhood of 100,000 hours of psychotherapy throughout the last three decades, resulting in a brand new slogan: "Psychotherapy. There is no substitute."

Power Tool #2: Guided Imagery
Healing happens inside.

—Andrew Weil

After facilitating all of those hours of psychotherapy, I believe that no tool or technique is more important or more valuable than guided imagery.

As I have stated repeatedly, in order for humans to heal from emotional pain and trauma, there must be appropriate closure or cleansing of the psychological wound. As pointed out in *Your Mind: An Owner's Manual for a Better Life*, time, in and of itself, does not provide that healing, it merely passes. Healing is active and requires letting go of the pain. To do so, however, most often we need to revisit the painful incident(s) or material in order to feel, express, and finally release it.

And that's where guided imagery becomes such a powerful ally and tool. You see, with guided imagery, you can safely return to unfinished scenes from an earlier chapter of your life and release whatever has been haunting you for so long. What kinds of painful things can we lay to rest? Scenes of sexual abuse and childhood trauma, adult rape, saying goodbye to departed loved ones, confrontation of bullies and abusers, combat-related traumas, automobile accidents, and so on. *There is no trauma that cannot be addressed effectively* with guided imagery.

Your only requirements as client/patient are: 1) the ability to relax from the induction of the therapist, 2) the ability to visualize any scenario introduced by the therapist (even imagining a spotted pink elephant with closed eyes, for example), and 3) the courage to face the disturbing stimulus.[1]

In a two-week period recently, I utilized the guided imagery power tool on four different cases with remarkable success: a 69-year-old man said goodbye to his brother who died in Vietnam 45 years earlier; a 55-year-old woman released the nightmare of a rape she suffered at the age of 20; a man healed the emotional component of a head-on accident between an automobile and a motorcycle; and Amy, a 33-year-old woman, released the trauma of "killing my best friend, Julie" in an auto accident at the age of 19.

I'd like to share Amy's story: she presented two years earlier with symptoms of traumatic brain injury (TBI) including impulsivity, irritability, substance abuse, reckless behavior, volatile relationships—you get the idea. She set out to change all of that by investing in a therapeutic relationship with me for two sessions per month. To my amazement (and I think hers, too) she decided to quit drugs, promiscuity, and petty theft in favor of enrolling in college to become, of all things, a therapist.

But even with scholastic success and the aforementioned behavioral changes, Amy was still suffering silently from symptoms of Post Traumatic Stress Disorder, including intrusive recollections of the fatal accident and a bucket load of accompanying anxiety. She also marinated in toxic guilt because she was driving under the influence of drugs and alcohol when she swerved off the road and into a tree. It was hard for Amy to feel fortunate that she lived and Julie did not.

One day Amy revealed that she was suffering from these symptoms even after 15 years. I asked her if she was ready to put them away with guided imagery. She didn't understand the technique or how and why it works, but she did know that she wanted to feel better and that she could trust me.

I induced relaxation (see relaxation response) and took her to an imaginary, empty movie theater where she and I sat. I gave her a remote that worked to control the movie on the big screen, with the ability to hit play, stop, rewind, fast-forward, and so on. We went back to the accident, to watch it one more time and "put it away forever." She was allowed to minister to an ailing Amy. We then afforded her an opportunity to speak and listen to her friend who was granted the opportunity to visit Amy one more time from the beyond. I spoke for Julie and related, "While I am not permitted to reveal anything about the beyond, I can tell you that I am happy and well and have long since forgiven you. My only request is that you forgive yourself and live your life to make a difference."

None of this happened, of course, except in the sanctity of Amy's head. But she cried and cried tears of release from her emotional prison and put the accident and Julie's death in a place where it no longer haunted her. To hear Amy tell it, "I'm done. It's over. I finally have peace."

In fact, the anniversary date of the accident was December 1st. But for the first time since it happened, Amy no longer anticipated the date only to suffer through it. In fact, she forgot all about it until she realized on December 4th that it had passed peacefully. She believes that Julie would be as pleased as she is.

Did you know that the technique called Reiki is effective with older adults in decreasing pain, depression, and anxiety? This is a healing technique in which the therapist can channel energy into the patient by touch, to activate the natural healing processes of the patient's body, and restore physical and emotional well-being.[2]

Power Tool #3: Successive Approximation
Worry often gives a small thing a big shadow.

—Swedish Proverb

Eight-year-old Tamika was one of the most delightful patients I've ever had the honor of treating. Maybe it was her disarming smile; more likely, it was the way she took over the office when she arrived, always taking time to ask the other patients in the waiting room, "Why do *you* come here?"

Tamika knew why her mom brought her to see me—she was chased, caught, and thrice bitten by two unleashed Dalmatians. While the horror of the attack lasted less than a minute, the impact on Tamika was profound: she was now generally anxious, hyper-vigilant (overly watchful), and far less spontaneous than the little third-grade president was prior to the attack. And, needless to say, she was now *petrified* of dogs of any kind. To Tamika, an 18-year-old dachshund with an artificial hip was now transformed into a Bengal tiger with an attitude.

My job description was simple, according to Tamika: "Can you make me like dogs again?" Of course, I was tempted to say, "If I could do that, I could also make you like broccoli and homework." But, instead I related, "Together, sweet girl, we could do anything you strive to do."

Overcoming phobias, as you'll see in the subsequent chapters, is rarely easy, but *they are treatable*. The treatment of choice for Tamika is called successive approximation, a fancy term for taking one step at a time. Or, more accurately, one successful step at a time. The idea behind this technique is to succeed in small steps until the final goal is realized.

Just as in the technique of systematic desensitization (see Power Tool #4 on page 106), the duo of psychologist and client team up to create a step-by-step list of goals, each one progressively more challenging and/or frightening. The goals can be achieved by utilizing any number of techniques from guided imagery to in vivo (real life) exposure to the feared object or situation. Tamika and I also used psycho-education, teaching her appropriate approaches to strange dogs and modeling the safe handling of dogs. We created a 1 to 10 hierarchy, beginning with thinking about a puppy being born in Australia (I suggested that the puppy be born on the moon, but she said that was impossible, due to "atmospheric conditions"). Our progression included an in vivo visit with Nate, my less-than-vicious 7-pound Maltese. We also had Tamika imagine successful encounters with increasingly larger dogs, and she also learned how to present her hand to strange dogs, even if they were barking excitedly. She breezed through the steps, one-by-one, much to the delight of her mother and shrink.

> Did you know that animal-assisted therapeutic recreation sessions had a significant effect in reducing average anxiety levels of people with mood disorders?[3]

Our final goal was prompted by a contact I had in the K-9 unit of the local police department. I figured if Tamika could master the challenge of petting a huge beast of a German Shepard, she could potentially return to her pre-morbid state of enjoying dogs with appropriate caution for the strange ones. It was a brilliant plan, if I said so myself. There was no way it could possibly fail. Except for the one way it failed miserably.

There we were, Tamika; Charlie, the K-9 officer; Rocket, a Shepard the size of a German tank; and me. There was lots of love and affection in the room, culminating in Tamika tenderly stroking Rocket with the confidence of a lion tamer. We had reached level 10. She was cured!

Just at the moment when I was about to high-five myself for a brilliant treatment plan, Rocket lunged toward the window, exploding in a barking frenzy! Two men were outside my office attempting to wash my windows—naturally, no one had washed those windows in the five years I had rented—and alarmed Rocket to the point of provoking his death growl. Tamika was petrified and regressed back down the scale to the Australian puppy. Her psychologist was of little help from his vantage point, hiding under the couch. Charlie jumped in and settled Rocket down, but the damage was already done.

If every cloud has a silver lining, we were able to locate that lining in the subsequent session. The resilient Tamika was able to proceed through the hierarchy very quickly the second time; the learning was not lost! Charlie and Rocket returned to find a confident young lady who benefited from her close-up with the protective Rocket, and realized that having police dogs were good for society and not bad for her. She learned to feel safe with most dogs and how to appropriately handle the strange ones. According to her mom, the child she knew before the attack was alive and well, with a tad more confidence and a plan to become a psychologist one day.

> Patients with Panic Disorder experience the best outcomes with a combination of behavioral treatments: exposure, relaxation training, breathing techniques, homework tasks during treatment, and participation in a follow-up program. Overcoming your panic permanently requires diligent follow-through and practicing all your new skills.[4]

Power Tool #4: Systematic Desensitization

When you change the way you look at things, the things you look at change.

—Wayne Dyer

Here in Southwest Florida, there is so much to be proud of. For instance, each year we boast the highest number of lightning strikes in the entire world. Although this can be perilous to golfers, swimmers, and Ben Franklin impersonators, it's good for psychologists. Each year, we can expect a little new business created by a stray lightning bolt or an explosive summer storm.

Alice, this year's storm survivor, had her own harrowing story: the deluge created by an afternoon downpour wreaked havoc upon a local highway, contributing to a rear-end collision and a newborn fear of summer storms. As is often the case, Alice generalized the bad afternoon on the road to anytime she could hear the rumble of thunderclouds in the distance. In other words, Alice was afraid to drive virtually every afternoon of the entire summer! Needless to say, this was dreadfully inconvenient and frustrating for Alice. As you might imagine, her preference was to schedule appointments early in the day, so as to avoid the potential of driving during the afternoon thunderstorms. Avoidance is the great enabler of all fears and phobias.

But phobias are treatable (or I might have written a book on arranging hydrangeas instead), so I introduced Alice to the power tool called systematic desensitization. A fancy, clinical phrase with a simple premise: take an anxious/phobic person and teach them to relax. While they are relaxed, lying eyes-closed on your couch, walk them through a 10-step progression from least scary to most scary image. So, in Alice's case, she selected a progression (also known as systematic units of distress or SUDs) that began with 1—pulling out of her driveway—and ended with 10—driving in pouring rain on a major highway.

You see, when you are relaxed and imagine experiencing a certain scary scene, your nervous system can break the bond between anxiety and that very scene and replace it with relaxation. So Alice could imagine driving in the rain while relaxed and laying on my couch, and, after enough practice, she could do it in vivo (real life). That's how systematic desensitization works.

We begin with a relaxation exercise and then proceed with the first unit (the driveway) and imagine driving it. We then move to the second, third, and beyond, one unit at a time. (The rule of thumb is not to move more than three units in any given practice session.) If the patient gets a little anxious while imagining the scene, we go back to relaxing and retreat to the previous scene. When ready, we return to that same scene and hope for more relaxation the next time. Eventually you can master the greatest fear—the 10th unit of distress—while being relaxed. Of course, after succeeding on the couch, the goal is to overcome the scary scene in vivo.

Alice appeared one Thursday in July for a 3 p.m. session—it was the only appointment available—and relaxed quickly on my third-story couch by the window. It didn't take long before my suggestion that she imagine a thunderstorm became very easy to accomplish. Evidently, Mother Nature was also listening and responded by contributing an in vivo thunderstorm right outside my window, while Alice closed her eyes and imagined driving in the midst of the storm.

The two ladies (Alice and Mother Nature) combined for a very effective session. Alice was able to proceed successfully to the 8th unit of distress, leaving only the rain-soaked drive on the major highway for our next session. She accomplished her goal and took back control of her driving and her Florida summers.

Sometimes, nature is a real mother. Other times, it's a nurturing parent.

Complementary alternative medicines are making a significant impact in our healthcare system. These alternative approaches are becoming more commonly used by doctors, chiropractors, and physical therapists, who are implementing them in their everyday practices. One primary alternative is massage therapy, which has shown to be effective in aiding the ease of stress, anxiety disorders, and depression. Massage therapy promotes relaxation and studies have shown it can balance the autonomic nervous system and increase the parasympathetic branch, which signifies a rest-and-digest response. Massage has been proven to reduce the stress hormone cortisol, which promotes calmness and alleviates anxiety and depression. Moreover, massage can increase the neurotransmitters, serotonin, and dopamine.[5, 6]

Tool #5: Exposure and Response Prevention (ERP)

If you've been paying attention to popular media you've noticed a significant increase of awareness of mental disorders, like schizophrenia, bipolar disorder, post-traumatic stress disorder, and attention deficit/hyperactivity disorder (ADHD). You've also seen television specials focused on agoraphobia, hoarding, and even obsessive-compulsive disorder (OCD). The latter has also been featured in the behavior of some rather popular characters on TV (*Monk*) and in movies (Jack Nicholson's character in *As Good As It Gets*). We laugh at the absurdities of the characters' rituals and agree with Helen Hunt when she sees Jack walking in the street to avoid stepping on a crack and says, "This is not going to work for me."

Is there a disorder anywhere that undermines one's progress by interfering so powerfully into all aspects of life than OCD? Is it even treatable? So far, we know what doesn't work: insight-oriented psychotherapy. We do know that medication works marginally, but the treatment technique that works best for OCD is a behavioral technique called exposure-response prevention. ERP, discovered originally by UK psychologist Victor Meyer offers consistently more successful outcomes for OCD than anything else currently researched.

ERP, as the term implies, exposes you to what you are most afraid of while preventing you from avoiding or escaping it. When you remain exposed to that feared object or stimulus for a prolonged period of time, behavioral psychologists say you will habituate (become accustomed) to that stimulus and extinguish the fear response (it goes away).

Naturally, the tendency for you, the average OCD sufferer, is to avoid/escape the moment your anxiety fires up. The same is true for you phobics. Like the Gingerbread man, you run away as fast as you can to gain relief. But with ERP, the escape route is closed or prevented. You are not allowed to run; you must face your fears!

Sergio was a very well-liked guy in college who had the misfortune of having me as a friend. While this was probably never a wise choice socially, it was especially foolish to call me "friend" when I was studying experimental psychology.

YARD BUNNIES

Dr. Laurie Ann O'Connor

I have yard bunnies. They come freely into my yard, uninvited, and they leave hopping away as well. I know for a fact that even people who have built pretty good fences around their properties still end up with yard bunnies. But just because they come into my yard does not mean I have to do anything with them.

Your thoughts are very much like my yard bunnies. Just because the bunny hopped into my yard does not make it my bunny. If, however, I capture the bunny, hold the bunny, feed the bunny, talk to the bunny, or nurture the bunny in anyway, I have taken some degree of ownership over the little creature. Instead of simply observing the bunny, I choose to interact with it. I become invested in it.

But what if I just let the bunnies be? Bunnies have been on this planet much longer than I have or ever will be. What if I do nothing? The bunnies will go on as they always have.

Your brain is like my backyard. There are, no doubt, many bunnies hopping in and out. Some may return while others make such a fleeting appearance that you were not always certain you actually saw a bunny.

It may help to learn to sit quietly and observe the bunnies before doing anything with them. You are being more thoughtful—more mindful—of what your actions will actually bring about. This is one of the many gifts that mindfulness meditation has for you. Rather than a knee-jerk, impulsive, or compulsive reaction to the bunnies hopping in and out of your yard, take a brief pause. Choose a moment to be mindful. After all, anxiety is like trying to keep a bunch of these bunnies. Panic is when it feels like the bunnies are taking over! Mindfulness is allowing my backyard to be at peace.

You see, Sergio was well known for being very OCD (and a tad claustrophobic)—his head-tapping and toilet flushing rituals were legendary in the guys' dorms. He had a Western Civilization class on the 9th floor of the Miller building, junior year. Sergio was OCD about most things, including prompt arrivals for appointments, and especially class. But with claustrophobia, there was no way he would even *consider* riding the elevator to the 9th floor. I mean, what if he got stuck?

Also a health fitness nut, climbing nine floors was not a problem for Serg. He just left 15 minutes earlier than the rest of us for Western Civilization. But one day I had an idea—one I'd quickly blame on Rob, my partner in crime in experimental psych. What if the staircase was "closed" one day and forced Sergio to take the elevator to the 9th floor? Rob was so excited by the image of seeing Sergio start his head-tapping ritual, he high-fived me in victory. That was all I needed to inspire me to borrow an orange cone from Tom, the custodian, and create a somewhat convincing sign that read: "Stairwell out of order. Please use elevator." I guessed that no one had ever used those words before in the history of elevators.

While one orange cone and a silly, homemade sign would not deter most people from scaling these steps, Sergio was a stickler for rules and he did not argue with umpires. "Rules are rules," he'd say.

Now, I know some of you are feeling anxious right about now, wondering if this deceptive, inhumane experiment is even ethical for psychologists. Please rest assured that our prank/experiment was cruel, highly unethical, and completely inappropriate for psychologists. Fortunately, however, we were only college students and not real psychologists at the time.

So, we hid in a nearby office and watched out the window as poor Serge read and re-read the sign, sighing and throwing his hands up in the air, two, three, seven times. We roared in silent laughter. He walked back and forth from stairs to elevator and back again, until finally he made his decision—he was going to class now, so he wouldn't be late. He took one final deep breath, entered the elevator, and took off for class.

Rob and I looked at each other in disbelief; Sergio was boarding an elevator! What if we killed him? We charged out of the classroom, made a bee-line to the stairwell, and ran up nine bleeping flights of stairs in an effort to catch Serge coming out of the elevator. But it was too late. Serge was already seated comfortably in class, no indication that he'd just completed the ride from hell! Rob and I, on the other hand, were hopelessly out of breath and looking a bit suspicious.

Sergio was a lot of things, but not stupid. He quickly put the pieces together and realized that he was victimized by two 20-year-old pranksters who admired him as much as they enjoyed teasing him. Instead of retaliating, he wrote us a little note soon after, one we won't soon forget. It read:

Hey you two wannabe shrinks! I know about your little prank. I was about to retaliate, when my late father's words kicked in! He said, "Son, the best revenge is always success." How true. I learned that day that I needed to face my fears and stop running from them. I've been using the elevator successfully ever since. And I owe it all to you two shitheads. Thanks guys!

Rob and I didn't know whether to laugh or cry. Mostly we felt a little guilty and embarrassed. And very proud of Sergio. We also learned a little something about the power of ERP that day (and a lot about ethics).

> We now have research indicating that by combining different cognitive/behavioral techniques like exposure, systematic desensitization, successive approximation, and in vivo modeling, patients could experience significant improvement in only one, three-hour-long session! Their promising results were demonstrated successfully on children, adolescents, and adults in international venues.

Power Tool #6: Relaxation, Yoga, and Mindfulness

Rest and relaxation (R&R); it's what you work for, save for, live for. But do you really know how to relax? Chances are, you require a substance (alcohol), or perhaps a destination (the beach), or more likely, a combination thereof (a piña colada on Siesta Beach) to help launch you into relaxation mode. But what if you could learn to relax—really relax—in your own home? Every day? Without the chemicals?

I know, I sound suspiciously close to an infomercial that will say something like, "Well now you can!" And soon after, I'd throw in some ginsu knives to seal the deal. Take heart, this is not an infomercial, its scientific research. And the research says this: if you can give up 15 minutes of your day to practice relaxation (of your choice), you might see the following results: a significant reduction in anxiety, blood pressure, physical pain, tension headaches, and cortisol (the stress hormone). You will notice an increase in sleep quantity and quality, a reduction in the likelihood of suffering from cognitive decline (dementia), depression, and perfectionism. Also, presumably a significant improvement in sexual function. With all of this, who needs knives?

Relaxation retrains your nervous system to respond with calmness, instead of igniting the stress response and creating anxiety. The daily practice, of course, guarantees that you become proficient at relaxing, so much so that it becomes your initial response, your first line of defense. Imagine walking around your life in relaxation mode, instead of chronically anxious and one stressor away form a major melt down!

But how does one relax with the myriad issues present in the life of John Q. Public and his lovely wife Jane? The answer, of course, is to find a relaxation exercise that works for you. Let's explore a few different options among the many relaxation exercises available. We can start with a Harvard-trained psychologist named Herbert Benson, who created a technique called the *relaxation response*. The idea was to help people to respirate deeply enough to reduce their breathing rate, pulse, and even cognitions. His technique caught on quickly and spread like wildfire.

Benson defined relaxation as "a state of decreased Psychophysiological arousal: a calming state."[7] An excerpt of Benson's method is included below:

Sit quietly in a comfortable position.

Close your eyes.

Relax your muscles, progressing from your feet to your calves, thighs, abdomen, shoulders, head, and neck.

Breathe slowly and naturally. As you do, repeat the word "One" silently to yourself as you exhale.

Assume a passive attitude. Don't worry about how well you're doing. When other thoughts come to mind, simply say to yourself, "Oh well," and gently return to your repetition.

Continue for 10 to 20 minutes.

Do not stand immediately. Continue sitting quietly for a minute or so, allowing other thoughts to return. Then open your eyes and sit for another minute before rising.

Practice the technique once or twice daily. Good times to do so are before breakfast and before dinner.[8]

> Relaxation techniques proved to be effective in reducing anxiety for people of the general population as well as for people with physical or psychological disorders. Its effectiveness was noted, whether used as a separate technique or used with other types of treatment.[9]

But there is more than one way to skin a cat. Edmund Jacobsen was not content to just lie around breathing heavily. That type of relaxation was evidently too easy for him, so he devised a hard-working relaxation, complete with tight, flexing muscles of all kinds. Although never billed as such, it was obviously the relaxation of choice for real men.

He taught his protégés to tighten and flex their major muscle groups, holding the flex for five seconds before releasing. The result is a tired, relaxed muscle, one that falls into relaxation by contrast after the five-second flex. An excerpt of Jacobsen's progressive muscle relaxation is included below:

Think of it as if you were getting certain skills, like bike riding, which will help you in the future.

Try to find a quiet place, isolated from any noise that would distract you. In order to facilitate the relaxation, the temperature of the room should be comfortable—neither too hot, nor too cold—and illuminated by a dim light.

Find a comfortable outfit—not too tight. Take off glasses, bracelets, etc...

You can lie on a bed and spread your arms and legs out slightly. Or you can also sit on a comfortable couch, preferably with arms. Make sure you lean your neck, shoulders, and back appropriately and comfortably.

If you lose focus or experience some intrusive thoughts during the relaxation process, don't try to fight them, but instead let them go.

Now close your eyes.

Take 5 deep breaths, inhaling through your nose and slowly letting your breath out through your mouth. Repeat this procedure five times.

After this deep breathing repetition, continue breathing in a slow and paused manner, but at a normal pace.

From now on, every time you breathe in, repeat the phrase "hold it" and every time you breathe out, repeat the word "easy."

With this continuous repetition, the words will come out rhythmically, along with the rhythm of your breathing, and the relaxation becomes deeper and deeper.

The dense of well-being and profound calmness increases and develops itself... "hold it"... "easy"...

Continue in this manner a little longer. Keep your eyes closed, but following the rhythm of your breathing in and out, keep sounding out the words "hold it" and "easy."

Now tense forcefully all the muscles in your body. All the muscles will now become tight and tense.

Now tense forcefully the following muscles:

- Legs: tense energetically...let go. Breathe.
- Thighs: tense energetically...let go. Breathe.
- Glutes: tense energetically...let go. Breathe.
- Pelvis: tense energetically...let go. Breathe.
- Abdominal: tense energetically...let go. Breathe.
- Back: tense energetically...let go. Breathe.
- Chest: tense energetically...let go. Breathe.

- Neck: tense energetically...let go. Breathe.
- Jaw: tense energetically...let go. Breathe.
- Forehead: tense energetically...let go. Breathe.
- Shoulders: tense energetically...let go. Breathe.

Let go of all the tension and relax completely. Feel the immediate well-being sensation.[10]

Just in case you are still uptight, how about we introduce another method of learning relaxation, a technique called biofeedback. Long a staple in health psychology, this technique has been utilized to treat everything from tension headaches and hypertension to attention deficit. Neurofeedback, a close cousin of biofeedback (they attend the same family reunions), places a greater emphasis on improved imaging technologies that allow you to see what exactly is going on—where and when. Neurofeedback is a newer, less-studied technique, but the research available at this time is promising, especially for the treatment of anxiety disorders.

The goal of these procedures, as you might guess, is to induce significant relaxation by helping you to place your focus on stimuli other than your pain, tension, or blood pressure. As your concentration increases, you are capable of ushering in the same relaxation response proffered by Benson and Jacobsen. But with bio/neurofeedback, you benefit from a machine that provides cues (sounds, sensations, or visual images) as to whether what you are doing is actually reducing or increasing your tension, heart rate, respirations, and so on.

Recall the hot and cold game from childhood, when your best friend is trying to locate the cool sunglasses you stole and hid in your room. When she moves closer to them, you say, "getting warmer," when she turns in the wrong direction, you say "ice cold!" The cues in biofeedback guide you in the direction of total relaxation.

Finger Dot Story

Of course, there are other methods of relaxation, including yoga, meditation (including transcendental meditation), and hypnosis. There is also a concept called mindfulness, which is a practice that incorporates all of the previously mentioned relaxation methods into a comprehensive approach toward taming anxiety. But I'm getting ahead of myself...perhaps I should just relax.

Not long ago, I had the opportunity to present to a Parkinson's support group on the subject of anxiety. We discussed many of the topics presented in this book, including mindfulness, social connectedness, exercise, sleep, and so on. During the presentation, I placed a small temperature-sensitive sticky dot on the fingertips of each of the participants. The point of the exercise was to demonstrate how each person's cognitions (thoughts, attitudes, beliefs) directly influenced their physiology. One particular gentleman observed how warm his hands were—his dot turned a brilliant, deep blue, indicating that he was indeed very relaxed. But at the end of the presentation, he wandered over to me complaining that his dot wasn't working, as it turned from deep blue to a forest green, for no good reason. The green, I reminded him, suggested that he was now more stressed. "Impossible," he stated emphatically. "I enjoyed the presentation. All I did was get up to leave. There is no need to be stressed." "Okay, well, what were you just thinking?" I asked. "Oh, wait," he smiled sheepishly, "I was just thinking that I have to pick up my wife on the way home. I hate that she always tries to tell me how to drive."

From head to toe, to the tips of our fingers, your mind and body are one.

Mindfulness

Each morning we are born again. What we do today is what matters most.

—Guatama Buddha

You don't need to learn to be mindful. You already know how to do it. You mastered it before you mastered potty training. Now you need to re-learn. My 2-year-old, Dylan, who had the misfortune of being born just in time for me to use him repeatedly in my analogies for this book, is very advanced in mindfulness. Whether he is stacking

Cheerios equally in both nostrils, overfeeding the Siamese fighting fish, or demanding that I read *Barnyard Animals Take a Bath* to him for the 47th consecutive time, he is living completely in the moment. He is *always* in the moment. He begins exactly no sentences with, "You know, Dad, when I was a kid..." He acts as if he is oblivious to the upcoming elections, doesn't fret about the potential of being an "undecided" major in college, or whether social security will even be there when he retires. He is a mindfulness zen master at 34 3/4-inches tall. And, according to Eckhart Tolle, author of the *Power of Now: A Guide to Spiritual Enlightenment*, "the master is totally at one with his movement."[11] It is unclear if he was referring to Dylan.

Mindfulness, like so many hot topics in 21st-century psychology, has its roots in ancient wisdom. Mindfulness is entering into the present without judgment. When you maintain focus on the now, you are incapable of replaying your past or worrying about the future because now is the only moment that exists.

You are probably familiar with the concept of "be here, now." For most humans, however, being in the here and now and not reliving past moments or thinking of future events is almost unnatural. We have been taught to dwell in the past by celebrating our victories and their anniversaries, or wallowing in our mistakes, presumably so we don't repeat them. Preparing for the future is also a mindset that we are exposed to. We learn to save for a rainy day or, as the boy scouts remind us, "always be prepared."

But true happiness, from what we understand, is lived in the now, the present moment. Let's check out some relevant quotations from some of the greatest teachers of all time:

"All that we are is the result of what we have thought. The mind is everything. What we think, we become."

—Guatama Buddha

"Take no thought for the morrow; for the morrow shall take thought for the things of itself."

—Jesus, as quoted in Matthew 6:34

"Each time you take a mindful step, you are back in the arms of Mother Earth and are reminded of your true, sweet home in the here and now."

—Thich Nhat Hanh

"We can never obtain peace in the outer world until we make peace with ourselves."

—the 14th Dalai Lama

"Nothing has happened in the past; it happened in the now. Nothing will ever happen in the future; it will happen in the now."

—Eckhart Tolle

"It is not uncommon for people to spend their whole life waiting to live."

—Eckhart Tolle

"The best time to plant a tree is 20 years ago. The next best time is now."

—Confucius

"I've never felt anxiety while in the moment. It's always been while [I've] had time to think about what is to come or time to reflect on what has been."

—David King, Olympic figure skater

"Oh yes, the past can hurt. But the way I see it, you can either run from it, or...learn from it."

—Rafiki, friend/advisor to Simba, in *The Lion King*

Although mindfulness-based stress reduction (MBSR) and cognitive-behavioral stress reduction (CBSR) may both be effective in reducing perceived stress and depression, MBSR may be more effective in increasing one's ability to stay in the moment, increasing energy and reducing pain.[12]

So there you have it from six spiritual leaders, one Olympic athlete, and a mandrill. But ancient wisdom, at times, is, well, ancient. And not always wise, with all due respect to the Flat Earth Society and Salem Witch Hunters. How does mindfulness (staying in the now) measure up when scientifically researched? Quite well, actually. According to the wealth of research on the scientific study of mindfulness, the following can be asserted with complete confidence in the here and now: people who practice the art of mindfulness-based stressed reduction (MBSR) have reduced blood pressure and blood sugar, reversed heart disease, lowered cholesterol, balanced hormone levels, reduced physiological symptoms of anxiety, strengthened immune functions, decreased perceived stress and depression, and increased energy levels. In fact, in a research study comparing the effects of mindfulness-based and cognitive-based stress reduction, the results indicated that although both approaches were quite effective, the mindfulness trained group enjoyed better outcomes with regard to energy, pain reduction, and decreased tendency for binge eating.[13]

Let me put it this way: If you knew a pill existed that could accomplish the above-mentioned list of health benefits—no, even half that list—wouldn't you take it? So what would stop you from learning to practice mindfulness?

Is it possible to *always* be in the moment? Not hardly. I'll bet Buddha brooded, the Dalai Lama lamented, and Jesus kvetched. I'm sure you will, too. But let me give you a rule of thumb that you might find helpful: if you leave the present in favor of the past, it had better be to recall helpful lessons or facts or to tell humorous stories. If you are stuck in the past in regret and/or resentment, you need to finish what is still undone for you (see Chapter 10).

If you leave the present for the future, it had better be to plan your daughter's wedding, not to worry if their children will inherit their father's pointy ears. Planning is healthy, worry is toxic. What if you are beset with a nagging worry? Note it, accept it, and then walk it to the door of your mind. If it returns, repeat the process. Do not try to not think about it, as it won't work. Did you ever try to not think about a white bear?[14]

Stay in today and relish each moment, because in reality what else do you have? One more quote:

"Practice mindfulness like there's no tomorrow."
—Dr. Christopher Cortman, underpaid psychologist.

Yoga

We have provided you already with several different styles of relaxation, including diaphragmatic breathing in Chapter 4, Benson's relaxation response, Jacobsen's progressive muscle relaxation, and bio/neurofeedback. And yet, we haven't even touched the age-old art and practice of yoga, despite the fact that yoga is an integral part of mindfulness-based stress reduction (MBSR) and has a well-established track record for effective treatment of anxiety. Giving yoga the mention it deserves, not only as a component of mindfulness, but as a lifestyle and health practice, would require a separate book devoted only to the many types and practices of yoga. Additionally, the effective practice of yoga far surpasses the skill level of three Western-trained psychologists, with all due respect to learning to do the downward-facing dog on Siesta Beach.

But for now, let's borrow a quote from the all-powerful Oz (Dr. Mehmet Oz), who states "proving yoga works is not the issue—now it is trying to determine how it works."[15]

Understanding how to meditate is another key to learning to practice MBSR. And, at the risk of stressing you out by providing you with another stress reduction relaxation exercise, may I present you with a basic mindfulness meditation?

Mindfulness Meditation

Begin this meditation by finding a posture or position that is comfortable for you. Sitting cross-legged on the floor is traditional and may be best, but it is important to try and find a position that you are generally comfortable in for 20 minutes or so. This position is often defined as comfortable yet upright, relaxed, and present. Notice the weight and touch of your body in this seated position. Notice what is here at this moment. Let your attention come to rest on your breathing. Your breath is your center and will always be the place you return your thoughts to if you find the need to refocus at any point.

Bring your awareness to the gentle rising and falling of your breath in your abdomen. You may also notice your breath as it flows in and out of your body. Notice the air as it enters your nostrils and your belly expands as you inhale. Feel the air gently leave your body as your belly softens. Be aware of your breath—one breath at a time. A single breath. What does this feel like in this very moment?

Frequently, other experiences will comes into your awareness, taking your mind away from your moment of the single breath. Many people find that they are very aware of sounds as they first practice. It may be traffic below in the street or a nearby dog barking at a passer-by. If you've forgotten to turn it off, it may even be your telephone. Whatever it is, listen to it until it no longer holds your attention and then return your focus to your breath.

You may feel your stomach growl or feel a bodily sensation that becomes stronger than your focus on your breath. When this happens, let go of your awareness of the breath and allow your attention and focus to be upon that sensation in your body. Notice if it lessens in intensity when you focus on it. Or perhaps if grows or shifts into another feeling. Again, when you are finished with that experience, bring your attention back to your breathing.

Researchers at Carnegie Mellon University found that as little as a single 25-minute mindfulness training session for three consecutive days resulted in significant stress reduction compared to people facing the same tasks but who had not had the training. In addition to the participants' subjective reports, the saliva samples all participants provided showed that the mindfulness training—just three sessions—resulted in a change in cortisol levels. Cortisol is often referred to as the *stress hormone*.[17]

Your breath is your home and your center. You may find your focus drawn to the exact moment when an inhale becomes an exhale. If you become aware of an emotion as you are sitting breathing, perhaps it is the emotion you ought to focus on. Specifically, feel where in your body that emotion is located or linked to. Notice if you feel any tension or tightness with it. Perhaps you may feel a trembling or vibrating. There are usually sensations to note when we are having an emotion. Observe and feel these in your body. Discover how you feel this emotion. Label it. Frustration? Fear? Anger? Sadness? Happiness? Once the emotion is no longer calling your attention, return to your breath. If there is something else calling your attention, let your mind go to that.

You will likely find that you are aware of thoughts in the background as you focus on your breathing. This is normal and okay. The goal of this mindfulness meditation is two-fold: to practice purposefully attending to one experience in the moment and to learning to intentionally let go of an experience (emotion, physical sensation, thought, and so on) and returning to a state of immediate presence. Unless the thoughts in your head grow larger and call your attention away from your awareness of your breathing, let them be. You may wish to label them as *thought* in the same way you labeled emotions. If you find that you have become lost in thought or are actively thinking and unaware of your breathing, label it with a word like *wondering* or *thinking* and return to your center. Return to your breath. This is your time to practice holding a singular focus. Give yourself permission to think later.

If you find that repetitive thoughts keep calling you away from your awareness of your breath, label them. Words such as *planning, worrying, remembering* will likely apply. There are no right or wrong labels. These are your thoughts. They are your labels. This is *your* practice.

The act of labeling often makes the thought disappear. If the thought remains, check with your body to see if there are bodily sensations with it that you can notice. Be curious about the thoughts and observe that they are. If, at any time, any of this feels uncomfortable or confusing, gently return your attention to your breath. In your awareness, regardless of whatever may be going on around you, you have the ability and focus to return to your breath. This is your center, your home, and a place you can always return to at will.

This is your experience. Relax into it. Be aware. Be curious. This is a way of exploring your own mind without judgment. Having an attitude of curiosity and openness will allow you to more easily integrate all of these experiences. You are witnessing your life unfold before you in a way that is new—moment-by-moment.

It is best to be in this mindfulness meditation for a few minutes at a time. Many people find it more difficult than they anticipated. If this is also your experience, continue anyway. Make the intention of adding a minute or two once you are comfortable at whatever time you have been practicing. While truly practice will never make perfect, patience is a gift of inner calm.

When you are finishing your practice, give yourself a moment to appreciate yourself. The following are traditional phrases used but always use what feels right for you.

May I be free from inner and outer harm and danger.
   May I be safe and protected.
May I be free of mental suffering or distress.
May I be happy.
May I be free of physical pain and suffering.
May I be healthy and strong.
May I be able to live in this world happily, peacefully, joyfully, with ease.

ANXIETY BUSTER

Visualization and Athletes
Dr. Harold Shinitzky, sports psychologist

You have finally achieved your dream. You walk on the baseball diamond. The green grass is like that of a country meadow. The size of the stadium is like the Roman Coliseum. You have worked diligently to earn the right to compete on the highest stage of your sport. Yet you experience a twinge of anxiety in the form of muscle tightness, worries, and thoughts that question your own skills.

Throughout the years of working with nationally ranked junior athletes to world class Olympic, professional athletes from every major association, I have found the mastery of visualization to be one of the most powerful tools in an athlete's training. I like to coordinate a three-skill intervention: deep breathing, muscle relaxation training, and visualization.

What is great about visualization is that it increases the neuro-circuitry connections between the brain and the body. Whatever your mind's eye sees is your reality. If you visualize the proper form your brain becomes accustomed and you develop muscle memory by rehearsing a successful outcome in that imagined situation. Muscle memory becomes more automatic the more you practice and master these steps. I recommend that each of my athletes practice the steps at least three times per day. Remember that you get better at whatever you practice. If you practice healthy thoughts, visualize how you will manage a future situation, and control your response to the event, you will see the progress. Individual athletic sports allow the focus on the singular athlete while team sports encourage the athlete to trust their teammates/partner and again focus on their individual's responsibilities. I like to increase the impact of this skill by tapping into all five of the senses. Realize the language utilized needs to fit the individual person/athlete/sport.

Let me use one case example of an Olympic pairs figure skater to illustrate how you can implement this into your daily routine. We begin as always with having the athlete get into a comfortable position with their head supported, eyes closed, and focus on their breathing/resting respiratory rate. We then progress to slowing their breathing pace down by taking deep breaths and, as they exhale, allowing their muscles to relax and unwind. Next, the powerful tool of visualization begins. I would ask my athlete to imagine themselves in practice. Imagine yourself at the rink. See the rink as a peaceful and quiet arena. Feel the cool sensation of the air as it invigorates your skin. As you breath in you can feel the chill in the air that is so familiar with your life as a skater. Remaining in this relaxed state, imagine yourself stepping onto the ice with your skating partner. You can trust your partner, as they too have put forth the massive required effort and training. You are in optimal physical shape from hitting the weights, stretching with yoga, fueling your body with proper nutrition, and committing to the long-term goal. You feel the excitement of the opportunity to practice and to do your best. You are confident and poised. As you skate to your center of the rink with your partner you anticipate the beginning of the music. As the music begins, you move as a well-choreographed pair in which two become one. As you perform your routine, you know what maneuvers await. See yourself sticking each move one at a time: a lift, a twist, a triple jump, your step sequence, and finishing in a beautiful death spiral. You neither under-rotate nor over-rotate. You glide from inside edge to outside edge with exacting precision. You feel strong yet graceful. You are powerful yet relaxed. You are confident to do your best but not cocky. As you take a deep breath in and fill your lungs to full capacity, you remain relaxed and focused, positive and aware. Tell yourself that you trust your coaching, you have the experience, and you have qualified and earned your spot in this event. I stay in the moment. I learn from my past. I don't worry about the future. I have the ability. Now is your time to shine. I am ready. My goal is to do my best.

I ask all of my athletes to practice deep breathing, muscle relaxation training, and visualization at least three times a day.

Now, imagine any situation in your life that you want to overcome and begin to practice visualizing how you will achieve your goal, control your response, perform up to your highest standards. Your gold medal awaits.

Phobias

He who fears he shall suffer, already suffers what
he fears.

—Michael de Montaigne,
The Essays of Michael de Montaigne, 1588

Fear is good. It keeps you from questionable decisions, like surfing on the roof of your drunken friend's jeep or sending a letter to the IRS stating: "Oh yeah? And who's gonna make me?" But phobias, by definition, are not only fears, they are irrational fears. They have no basis in reality.

Let me explain. I have no hard feelings toward slimy things, but I would prefer not to snuggle up with an amphibian on a cold, rainy night, if I can help it. I'm guessing that's pretty normal. But not Linda. She has a condition called batrachophobia—a fear of frogs—that is so debilitating, it influences every decision from where she parks her car to where she chooses to live. Just the mention of the word, *frog*, produces terrible anxiety and pained facial expressions. An amphibious intruder in her house provokes earth-shattering screams and a call to a neighbor who is charged with the task of locating and removing the now-petrified creature. It becomes a standoff. It's not easy being Linda, and its not easy being green.

Heart Attack vs. Panic Attack

According to the Centers for Disease Control, about every 25 seconds, an American will have a coronary event, and about one every minute will die from one. Every year about 715,000 Americans have a heart attack. Of these, 525,000 are a first heart attack and 190,000 happen to people who have previously had a heart attack.

The best way to tell the difference between a heart attack and a panic attack is to simply visit your doctor or emergency room for a heart test. More likely to be a heart attack: sensation of pain, or of pressure; tightness, squeezing, or burning; gradual onset of pain over the course of a few minutes; pain in diffuse area, including middle of chest; pain that extends to the left arm, neck, jaw, or back; pain or pressure accompanied by other signs, such as difficulty breathing, a cold sweat, or sudden nausea, and pain or pressure that appears during or after physical exertion or emotional stress or while you are at rest.

Less likely to be a heart attack: sharp or knifelike pain brought on by breathing or coughing; sudden stabbing pain that lasts only a few seconds; pain clearly on one side of the body or the other; pain that is localized to one small spot; pain that lasts for many hours or days without any other symptoms and pain reproduced by pressing on the chest or with body motion.[1]

Dr. Reid Wilson, MD From the Anxiety and Depression Association of America states, "Those who have never had a heart attack—but have been diagnosed with panic disorder and are fearful of a heart attack—should get a thorough physical evaluation to determine their heart health. If they are not at risk of a heart attack, then we begin the psychological work."

Corey is a rough and tumble guy. In fact, he's a 6-foot, 4-inch former marine. Currently, he spends his days hiding behind bushes and pulling people over for speeding as a state trooper. But Corey has a blinding and paralyzing fear of clowns, a condition known as coulrophobia. Like so many phobias, coulrophobia would not interfere with Corey's life very often, except for the fact that he works alongside a group of kind, sensitive men who are always looking to help Corey overcome his fears. As such, they do thoughtful little things like sticking stuffed clowns in his locker and wearing red noses and big shoes to work. On his birthday, they outdid themselves: Corey was very touched by the birthday cake in the private room, until the "Happy Birthday" song began and the man singing it was a paid clown from the local circus! Everyone roared with laughter, except the two men traumatized by the practical joke: Corey, and the man he nearly trampled on his charge out the door, the circus clown.

This is a real life example of the extreme volatility encased in a typical phobia. Think fear on steroids. But phobias, despite being highly treatable, are rarely treated because they usually don't tend to interfere with normal life. When they do, they can most often be avoided. Many of my patients, for instance, have suffered from ophidiophobia, the fear of snakes, but not a single one of them presented in my office for that reason. In fact, as common as this phobia is, I have never treated a patient for that reason. And there are many other such phobias that plague people enough to avoid situations and events, but never pursue treatment: Michael once fell off a bridge—it's a long story—but now suffers from gephyrophobia, a fear of crossing (and falling off) bridges, so he avoids them when he can. Sophie lost everything she owned in a tornado and now suffers from lilapsophobia—fear of tornadoes—so she re-located from Oklahoma to Florida. I don't have the heart to tell her about hurricanes. I (Dr. Cortman) suffer from acrophobia, fear of heights, or I would have elected to become a much taller man.

The Birth of a Phobia

Let's talk about how phobias form, as it appears that we are not born with phobias. If you can remember the classic research of Ivan Pavlov, the Russian scientist who, for some unknown reason, was fascinated with the saliva of dogs, we can begin there. A clanging bell, when paired with the stimulus of food, began to evoke the response of saliva from the dog's mouth. So by ringing the bell, the dogs would drool all over themselves. Soon, Pavlov realized he no longer needed to set out the food. The mere ringing of the bell would stimulate a full-blown salivating reaction.

Likewise, one slip off a sailboat could produce a fear of drowning that presents even at the *thought* of entering the ocean. One dog bite or canine attack could render the daintiest puppy into a blood thirsty Rottweiler. Similarly, one painful breakup could create a fear of commitment, a condition known as kakorraphiophobia. (Go ahead, take a moment to practice saying this one to your love of three years: "If you weren't so damn kakorraphiophobic, maybe we could have a future....") Hence, the fear produced by a single incident becomes associated with the general category of bridges, oceans, dogs, or even commitment to a partner, to produce an intense and irrational fear known as a phobia.

Treating a Phobia

So, once a phobia is born, it has the opportunity to grow and develop into a powerful entity. How? It becomes reinforced every time you think of it, feel the accompanying fear, and then avoid it. Remember that avoidance provides great relief and affords you a wonderful return to peace, tranquility, and deep breathing. Stay away from the encounters with that fear-inducing stimulus and you are fine. Confront the stimulus or even think about doing so and the anxiety skyrockets through the ceiling. When you think of it in this way, it's an easy choice. And so your phobia grows with every avoidance.

> Research reveals that people with social anxiety disorder, who participated in a 12-week treatment program featuring cognitive-behavioral therapy (CBT), experienced physical changes in their brain. These changes coincided with positive therapy outcomes. Stated succinctly, this is your brain; this is your brain on therapy.[2]

But if at any point you recognize the need to overcome your phobia, there is hope. Again, phobias are highly treatable. So let's take a close-up view of Jen, a 21-year-old woman who had successfully avoided boarding an airplane for the first two decades of her life. Jen was petrified of air travel, not because of a previous bad experience at 35,000 feet, but rather the many horrible catastrophes she *imagined* might befall her.

Jen might have staved off air travel for another couple of decades—she attended a local college and would drive and/or cruise on vacation—except that she had a once-in-a-lifetime offer from a college acquaintance: for the cost of air fare and whatever she might want to eat, she could experience Europe, specifically England, France, and Italy, with free rooms and personal guided tours. It was too enticing for Jen to pass up; she knew it was time to confront her phobia. The very first ingredient in overcoming any phobia is the motivation to do so. Jen was ready.

We began, of course, by discussing her feelings, from terror to excitement, and a plan to attack her phobia head on. I related that we would try a comprehensive approach (one that borrowed the tools of Chapters 4 and 5) to overcome her pteromerhanophobia. No matter how difficult our work would be, I reassured her, it would be easier than either 1) driving to her European destination or 2) pronouncing her phobia. Jen agreed.

The first tool employed was Jacobsen's progressive muscle relaxation (see Chapter 5), one of the most popular types of relaxation induction. Jen practiced tightening and relaxing her major muscle groups to learn how to be conscious of her tendency to stress herself and to gain expertise in deliberately relaxing her body. Jen liked the exercise, because she wanted to become proficient at pushing her own "relax" button instead of the more oft employed, "freak out now!" button.

When she reached some level of expertise, we labeled her Jenmaster, because she was now gaining confidence in her capacity to relax and because it rhymed nicely with Zenmaster, which she thought was cool.

Next, I introduced Gary Emery's brilliant concept of focus = energy, reminding her that, despite the fact that she was seated in an airplane, Jen could be anywhere she chose to be, anywhere she picked her focus. For example, if she decided to read a tour book, she could already be in Paris; if she opted to converse with her neighbor to the left, she could enter the life of a complete stranger; if she hopped on the internet, she could rub her trip into the nose of her ex-boyfriend. Jen elected Sudoku as the place where she would focus her energy. Hence, any challenging moments on board could be re-directed into the pursuit of numbers

1 through 9. Additionally, Jen added music as an alternative option to distract her from anxiety-inducing thoughts. She was beginning to realize that she could focus anywhere, anytime, on anything she chose. Anxiety would not attack her; she would have to create it by thinking catastrophic thoughts of entrapment and horror!

> Did you know that the virtual world may provide some help coping with specific phobias? An alternative approach to therapy that puts you face-to-face with your real-life feared situation is Virtual Reality Exposure Therapy (VR). The real power may be due to the fact the most people would prefer VR over real-life exposure.[3]

More rational thinking skills were employed, including taking a base rate on the likelihood that a plane crash would create her ultimate fear, death. We researched the probability and discovered that she was more likely to win the lotto, give birth to triplets, or be eaten by a great white shark than die in a commercial plane crash. We decided that there was probably a better chance that the shark would win the lotto and have triplets before she would go down, according to the data we discovered. Jen found that comforting also.

This led to cognitive restructuring exercises, made up of two parts: 1) catch yourself when negative internal comments begin and 2) insert a positive, constructive, productive comment based on reality. In other words, any thought like, "I just know something terrible will happen on this flight!" can be replaced by "I am so proud of myself for taking this flight and grateful that I have this amazing opportunity. I will enjoy every minute of this adventure including the flight overseas!"

> Did you know that there is now evidence from different countries that has shown the use of a One-Session Treatment (upward of three hours) can be effective in treatment and provide significant improvement in the lives of children and adolescents with specific phobias?[4]

All of these and other aforementioned tools were implemented, including mindfulness, replacing worry with faith, and letting go of all things that were not hers to control. We even equipped her with humorous scenes from her favorite TV show, *Southpark*, to prepare her in case she needed more deliberate distractions and efforts to change emotion. But then came the major power tool, *successive approximation*.

Successive approximation, as noted in Chapter 5, is the process of facing your biggest fear through a step-by-step formula. Often, it's a 10-step process, like the one we created together for Jen. Step one was a relaxed state in my office, followed by talking about flying, driving to the airport, going through the check-in process, and so on, until she reached the top fear: turbulence over the Atlantic.

We practiced all of this in imagery first (the technique called systematic desensitization—see Chapter 5) and then in vivo (real life). To ensure our success, Jen and I met in the airport parking lot one week, at the airport the next week, and then we met to do relaxation training on a friend's Learjet the next week. (It helps to have friends in high places.) Finally, my friend flew Jen and me for a half hour flight to create the closest simulation of her upcoming flight we could think of. Jen did well; the flight was uneventful. She seemed completely ready for her trip, which was only four days later.

I was in session on the day of Jen's flight when my cell phone made a noise to indicate a text message was received. After the session ended, I peeked at a picture of a smiling Jen standing with her friends at the top of the Eiffel Tower. The caption read, "Arrived safely in Paris. Please check my lottery ticket. Love, Jaws and the Three Baby Sharks."

ANXIETY BUSTER

Devon was a 47-year-old man in the midst of an ugly divorce. He was less than enamored with the antics of his soon-to-be ex-wife and her "blood-thirsty" attorney. He had recently started to "experience panic attacks" at the very thought of the upcoming legal process. So he decided to escape the nastiness and took a boys' trip on a cruise. He and his buddies took a "tubing" river adventure through a cave in Belize. Devon was having a great time until he heard a hissing sound and realized his tire tube had sprung a leak and was out of air. "I told my buddies, 'hey my tube is flat and they kept going down the river.' So there I was completely alone, in a pitch dark cave in the middle of bleepin' nowhere! My first thought was, so this is where it ends! I thought I might panic, but I remembered you saying panic never helps solve anything; it creates a problem."

"So what did you do?"

"That's just it. I didn't have a good plan to traverse the river without a tube, I knew it was too dangerous, so I just stood in ankle deep waters waiting for a brainstorm. And then, out of nowhere a river guide appeared with a brand new inflated tube for me. I was so proud of myself for not panicking and making things worse. You know what else brought me comfort? I knew even if I was stuck in that cave forever, at least my wife's attorney would never find me."

Take Home Messages:

1. All phobias begin with an association.
2. The most common (yet least beneficial) response is avoidance.
3. The healthiest coping skills address the phobia.
4. The best coping strategies usually include a range of garden or power tool approaches to decrease the physical reactions, as well as the thoughts and feelings.
5. Success over phobias occurs once the individual survives their worst fears and realizes it was based on their new, adaptive coping skills.

Exercises

1. The only thing to fear, is fear itself.

A. List any fears or phobias that you have.

B. When did you fears or phobias begin?

C. What occurred prior to the phobias that caused the fear?

D. What is the worst outcome that could happen?

E. In reality, what has been the worst outcome in your life regarding your phobia(s)?

Exercises (continued)
2. Life Beyond Phobias
A. List your fears or phobias.
B. How have your fears or phobias interfered with your life?
C. How would you feel if you could do all the things that your fears or phobias have prevented?
D. Describe how badly you would like to overcome your fears or phobias.

Exercises (continued)
3. Putting your past behind you.
A. List all of your fears or phobias.
B. List your personal variety of garden and power tools that you find to be helpful.
C. Create a record reviewing what tools helped to decrease your fears or phobias throughout the next several weeks.

Panic Disorder

As a rule, what is out of sight disturbs men's minds
more seriously than what they see.

—Julius Caesar

There you are, minding your own beeswax and WHAM! You are body-slammed with a peculiar, multi-system ambush that leaves you gasping for breath and wishing you completed your last will and testament. "What in the world is happening?" you ask yourself. Your chest is tight, heavy, constricted (some say that it feels as if an elephant is kneeling reverently upon their chest), your respiration is rapid and shallow—you can't catch your breath. You may have noticeable changes in your vision and hearing, tingling sensations down your arms and legs (paresthesias), nausea, queasy tummy, rubber knees, and a horrible sense that you are a) going to pass out; (b) losing your mind; (c) suffering a fatal heart attack; or d) all of the above. You are afraid you're dying and afraid you're not.

This "attack" lasts for minutes or (rarely) hours and completely drains you of today's energy supply and some of tomorrow's. It feels as if you've run a marathon and in a way, you have. You are spent, rattled, and still wondering if something is *very* wrong with your heart or mind. What you do know is that you've never felt this awful in your life and pray to God that whatever that was, it never, ever happens to you again. But you aren't the same after this episode. *You have just experienced your first panic attack.*

Your intentions are clear: you'd like to forget all about this experience and attribute it to stress, the heat, or your sister-in-law's meatloaf. But somehow you know it runs deeper than that. And rather than forget all about it, you can't help but think about your attack. Truth be told, you've become pre-occupied with it. Your family advises you to go tell your doctor, but you don't want to talk about this, as if talking about it will only fuel the inner beast.

And then it happens—you have another horrible attack! This time you go to the emergency room and after a three and a half hour wait, you are reassured that it's *only* a panic attack. You are prescribed a benzodiazepine and told to reduce your stress. Your heart is fine, no need to worry.

You don't want to be relying upon tranquilizers to make it through the day, but they do seem to take the edge off. And, truthfully, anything is better than experiencing another one of those attacks.

Over time, the attacks occur in what seems to be random places: the supermarket, a crowded restaurant, and the bridge you cross to get to work. Places that were normal and even pleasant before are now associated with feelings of anxiety, because having a panic attack there has contaminated them. Even when there is no panic you think that you may have an attack so there is no peace.

Every place where you have experienced panic is now a place you are inclined to avoid, if at all possible. You make excuses to get others to grocery shop, you are too busy to go out to eat, and eventually, you find a way to get your doctor to write a leave of absence note from work. Panic, for whatever reason, doesn't happen to you at home. You feel safe, in control, somehow insulated in an embryonic coating that allows you the very best chance to relax. You don't admit it to anyone, but you are going out of the house only sparingly these days. Each time you do, you can feel a sharp increase in anxiety and a dread that another attack is potentially imminent. At some point, not necessarily a date you circle on the calendar, you stop going out at all.

You are now suffering from panic disorder with agoraphobia.

Agoraphobia

So what in the world is agoraphobia? The word is derived from Greek and translates to "fear of the marketplace." But it isn't about the marketplace. In reality, it isn't about the movie theater, restaurant, bridge, or the car. It's not even about the boss, the coworkers, or the obnoxious friend of yours. It isn't about any of these things or people.

It's about panic attacks, also called anxiety attacks, or whatever your pet names for them are. For many, panic attacks are nothing short of debilitating.

But where do they come from?

Origin of Panic Attacks

According to the Diagnostic and Statistical Manual of the American Psychiatric Association, Fifth Edition (DSM 5), there are two different types of panic attacks: expected and unexpected. But I want to share some things that you may never hear/read anywhere else:

1. Panic attacks are a misnomer. They don't really attack you at all. Sorry, but it's not as if you are walking alone in the dark when out of the blue you are assaulted by a wild panic. Actually, you create your own panic.

2. Yes, as absurd as that sounds, it's true. Anxiety, as you have learned, is about the perception of threat. Panic is the perception of entrapment and/or loss of control. This is so critical, it bears repeating. Your so-called panic attacks are *created* by your perception that you are trapped and or out of control. You are petrified by your vulnerability, which triggers an exaggerated version of the stress response.

Let me explain: Sandra had never experienced panic until she heard the pilot's voice, "We are currently unable to obtain clearance for landing at this time. We will need to circle the airport." How could that audible message *create* a panic attack? How could any person's words create a physiological response within you? The pilot only wishes that his words contained the power to cause a disruption in a woman's physiology. The truth is, he doesn't have that power; if he did, all of the passengers would panic simultaneously. Instead, the only passengers who are affected by the announcement are those who are inclined to perceive themselves as trapped. And, just as quickly as panic wrapped its clutches into Sandra, the pilot grabbed the intercom microphone and stated, "Okay, we will be landing momentarily." Sandra's panic disappeared instantaneously, magically. Why? Because it only requires a nanosecond for Sandra's brain (or yours) to compute that there is no danger, no threat, no entrapment. The panic subsides.

> Did you know that in a recent study one in five patients in primary care practices had signs of anxiety? Unfortunately, only 61 percent of those with these symptoms were being treated. Their results indicated that 19.5 percent of the study patients in the primary care setting had one or more of the following: post-traumatic stress disorder, generalized anxiety disorder, panic disorder, or social anxiety disorder.[1]

3. Panic is not like cancer, AIDS, or even influenza. That is, if you worry about succumbing to any one of those illnesses, your worry will have zero impact upon your chances of contracting them. But not with panic. Just *thinking* about a panic attack can contribute to you creating one. Many of you know what I mean because you have already produced a panic attack just by worrying about the possibility of having one. How does that work? In much the same way you can recall anything else that is permanently stored in your brain. For instance, let's try something: close your eyes (not yet or you won't know what to do next) and listen to your mind replaying the song "Knock Three Times." You can hear it very well, even though it's not playing in your room, because it's recorded in your head. Can you smell an orange? Laugh at a scene from your favorite comedy? You have recorded all of these and many more like it in the hippocampus of your brain, which rapidly communicates with your limbic system and produces powerful feelings of humor, sadness, and yes, even panic, in a flash.

All of this to say you can re-create a full-fledged panic attack merely by thinking about how the panic felt and how terrible it would be to experience that again. "Oh no, here it comes again, please God, not now, not again!" Every one of those thoughts, in effect, pushes the panic button because they are *catastrophic* thoughts and produce the very symptoms that you most want to avoid. The more you fear having an attack, the more likely you are to create one. Think of yourself pouring gasoline on a fire in the effort to put it out. The fire increases, and so, in desperation, you pour more gasoline on the fire.

4. I'll bet the notion that you create your own panic attacks by perceiving entrapment and/or fearing the attacks sound like it is bad news. But it's not. It's actually good news in disguise. Why? It's simple. If you are the culprit, the one who causes all of this panic, you are also the one, the only one, who can put an end to panic and take your life back. Let's take a look at the story of Esther, the first lady of panic disorder with agoraphobia. A word of caution here before you read the story—if Esther can heal this disorder, there is no excuse for you.

Esther's Story

I have suffered with anxiety, panic attacks, and agoraphobia most of my adult life. Over twenty years to be exact. Throughout this time, panic and the accompanying body symptoms landed me in numerous emergency rooms. All neurological testing had negative results and the diagnosis was always the same: anxiety attack.

I was prescribed anti-anxiety medication, which offered relief with side effects. The culprit was always stress, which I did not deal with effectively. Self-medicating with alcohol seemed to work temporarily; however the withdrawal wrecked havoc with my neurological system only to worsen the panic. I was constantly waging war with panic. Obsessive, scary thoughts slowly took over. I spent more and more time planning my "escape route" and became a master at managing my anticipatory anxiety and avoidance behaviors. The "what ifs" were part of my daily dialogue. Driving alone, especially sitting in traffic, was always a sure bet for a full-blown attack. I could not escape, therefore I stopped driving. Soon, the only place I felt safe from panic and the impending doom was my home. I ventured out less and less and this was my new normal. This pattern of thinking took me years to cultivate.

I was able to work from home and soon my elderly father came to live with us. I had a new purpose, further justifying my agenda. These new boundaries kept me safe and I was controlling my panic. Venturing out to run errands was eventually possible with my so named "safe person," my husband, who would be at my side to rescue me should a new attack occur and save me from the inevitable doom.

No one knew what I was thinking and I convinced myself that this was normal for me. After all, I had my dad to take care of. This over thinking kept me emotionally drained and fatigued. Years ago, I was able to travel and drive alone in major metropolitan areas, never giving a thought to fear and panic. I yearned for the day that science would discover a cure.

My journey to recovery began in the spring of 2011. An advertisement, "Anxiety: The Common Cold of Mental Illness," in the local newspaper caught my attention. Despite the panic and body symptoms already kicking in, I was attending. The presentation by Dr. Cortman and Dr. Shinitzky was being held at the local hospital's auditorium. This was a comfort for me since surely the emergency room, should I require medical attention, was close by. I registered and now had a few weeks to plan my attendance and escape route. I already felt relief that I perhaps was going to find my cure. I did not sleep much. The anticipatory anxiety had taken over. My husband dropped me off early. I had to obtain an aisle seat closest to the nearest exit, so that I could easily flee, should the need arise. A good friend had also committed to be on "standby" should I need a ride if the panic I was planning for materialized. I was all set. Nothing should go wrong; I had spent hours obsessively planning my every move.

Miraculously, I thoroughly enjoyed the presentation panic free. My concentration shifted to listening to the psychologists. I could totally relate. I actually felt at ease and hopeful that I could be helped. At the end of the presentation, I approached Dr. Cortman, introduced myself, and stated that I suffered from panic and agoraphobia for years, and frankly, to this day, I can't explain where I obtained the emotional strength to ask for help. Dr. Cortman congratulated and hugged me for my attendance accomplishment. He asked me to call his office and make an appointment. I lived that day panic attack free, out of my comfort zone, surrounded by strangers. I was thrilled and felt confident that I could be helped to overcome this affliction. I will never forget that day. It was a new beginning for me.

I waited three weeks for my first session with Dr. Cortman. For me, attending that seminar was in itself a huge personal success. I could not stop thinking that I was capable of living life the way I felt so many years ago. With help, I told myself that I would do this. I had already learned that I was the cause of my anxiety and it was my perception of threat that resulted in panic. I referred to my seminar notes and what I found particularly true was that the nervous system does not know the difference between fact and fiction. It responds to my beliefs. My first indication of truth to this was that my focus shifted to the seminar presenters and I stayed panic free. To this day I always recall that belief in my internal dialogue.

In my first session with Dr. Cortman, I learned that I had to face my fears in order to overcome them. I fondly remember being told to "just sit in my car and drive out of the garage and into the driveway." Not letting the anticipatory anxiety set in, I went home and immediately proceeded with my new assignment. Nothing happened. No panic, so I continued to drive around the block. I stayed focused, applied my new thoughts, listened to my favorite tunes, and continued. I ended up at the local grocery store. I proceeded inside alone, to shop! I had not done that in years. Going down the aisles, I cried tears of joy. When I returned home, with groceries in hand, my husband was in shock. I actually ventured out alone and shopped. I couldn't wait to report back to Dr. Cortman. This was a huge accomplishment for me. I put all my faith and trust into Dr. Cortman's expertise, knowledge, and compassion. With my husband as president of my newly established fan club, I was on my way to recovery. Dr. Cortman became my coach. For the first time in healing this affliction, I had become accountable to someone. I was able to change my thought process and acquired new coping skills. I needed to stay focused in the present.

It's been three years since I began this journey. At times, it has not been easy, however, the rewards are too awesome for words. I no longer stress over everyday tasks. I have learned not to overanalyze every thought. I especially enjoy traveling again. Recently, I took a helicopter ride over the Grand Canyon. This was a personal goal I thought would never come to fruition. I gain emotional strength from every accomplishment. From my first drive out of the garage to a front seat helicopter ride; I will be forever grateful to Dr. Cortman.

So what was curative for Esther? Let's begin with her motivation to get better. What was her motivation after 20 years of suffering from agoraphobia? The same thing that motivates most people. According to James Framo, PhD, a highly renowned marriage/family therapist and my graduate school professor, "People don't change unless it's too painful not to."

For Esther, it had become too painful to do nothing. And to do nothing meant there would be no changes in her condition. To quote another professor, Dr. Robert Nay, "If nothing changes, then nothing changes." Remember: time doesn't heal, it merely passes. Twenty years was plenty of time. She was now frustrated, defeated, and quite desperate. She had motivation. So she showed up at our anxiety lecture and snatched us at the book-signing break. "After 20 years of being in my house, I saw your ad in the paper and I made it here today. Now one of you guys needs to help me, please." So we began our journey with a two-pronged homework assignment: "You bought our book (*Your Mind: An Owner's Manual For a Better Life*). Read it and do the exercises. Part two is simple: get in your car and back out of the driveway then back in."

"That's it?"

"That's it."

I was tapping into the several different tools from the onset. First, by reading the book, Esther was learning about the relationship between her cognitions and her emotions; that she created panic attacks by fearing their return. She would need to alter her thoughts about panic and I saw that she no longer needed to live in terror of panicking. Every cognitive tool we could muster would now be deliberately included in Esther's toolbox.

Another tool we were employing was the power tool of exposure. Remember, you never overcome your anxiety, fears, or phobias without facing them directly. Using exposure therapy, Esther would need to get behind the steering wheel and drive toward every scary road, highway, bridge, and destination.

We also utilized the power told of successive approximation, exploring baby steps such as: back out of your driveway and pull back in; drive around the block; drive to the highway, through town, and then turn home; drive the town highway for only one stoplight, and so on. Using this power tool is akin to entering the ocean up to your ankles, then out, knees, then out, and so on. Doing this correctly may involve the use of systematic desensitization exercises. (See Chapter 5.)

> Did you know that the presence of anxiety and substance use is a risk factor for the other? Anxiety disorders were significantly related to both alcohol and drug use disorders. Of note, Generalized Anxiety Disorder (GAD) and Panic Disorder (PD) with and without agoraphobia had the highest correlation with substance use disorders.[2]

Esther didn't seem to need to follow the treatment plan verbatim. In fact, she devoured the book and repeated helpful lines like they were her own private mantras. She quickly reached a place where the excitement of her successes was more powerful than the fear of creating a panic attack. The more confident and excited she became, the less she panicked. And predictably, the less she panicked, the more confident and excited she became.

Esther was not only skipping steps, she was leap-frogging over them. Within only four therapy sessions, Esther did the ridiculous—she scheduled a trip with "the girls" (three other adult women) to Germany. I wanted to tell her she was crazy, but it's not considered to be an appropriate response from psychologist to patient. I said little, because I neither wanted to discourage her efforts to win, nor make it seem like I thought it was a good idea. Ultimately, I let Esther take the lead on what she was ready for and what she wasn't. That turned out to be the most important positive I could provide Esther, with the possible exception of the tools and the encouragement.

Esther pieced together a mindset that could be summarized in the following manner: I create my own panic attacks by how I think. I will think differently. I am not trapped; I always have options. I choose to focus on my accomplishments and the challenges ahead. I have many skills to employ. I will no longer fear panic attacks. The less I focus on them, the fewer I experience. I can drive anywhere; I am a safe and competent driver. I will drive every day on roads and highways and across bridges. I am so proud of what I have accomplished. I will continue to grow by facing my challenges and fears for the rest of my life.

In the two years that I worked with Esther, she was able to accomplish all of her goals and became one of the most incredible patients I've ever worked with. She has taken no less than nine trips, including the European journey mentioned previously, Washington, Chicago, Boston, and New York state. She had driven across the Skyway Bridge, on interstates, and on to local islands that she had not been to. Fueled by her successes, she has also cured a gastrointestinal disease by changing her lifestyle and losing 45 pounds.

But all is not rosy in Esther-ville. Her husband wrote me a card stating, "Dr. Cortman, what have you done to my Esther? She is traveling around the country and world like she's on tour, spending weeks away and thousands of dollars. She can cross bridges to the barrier islands now and would love to live on the beach! I can't afford the new Esther! Is it too late to change her back?"

✗✗✗

So, you have panic attacks. How do you take back control of your life? Let's employ some tools from the previous chapters.

1. *Understand* that you are the source of your panic. You perceive yourself as trapped/overwhelmed. You are neither.

2. Talk back to yourself. Tell yourself panic "attacks" are not dangerous, merely uncomfortable.

3. The truth is, the less you fear these attacks, the less power they have. In some cases, as soon as people understand what they are (and aren't) and lose their fear, *they never experience another panic attack again!*

4. Remember your "A" words. *Approach* every nasty dragon of yours from bridges to public speaking, from crowded places to elevators, from restaurants to supermarkets, from movie theaters to interstate highways. Frequent these places to overcome the link between them and your panic response.

5. Speaking of "A" words, no more avoidance. Esther's amazing progress came only after she chose to take the necessary action to overcome the disorder.

6. Successive approximation is an important tool to utilize with your treating professional. But remember the principle is easy to employ on your own. Ride the elevator one floor only and then get off. Next time try two. It won't be long before you can ride it to the top of the Empire State Building.

7. Always remember investment plus threat. A reduction in the perception of threat will most often eliminate your panic attacks. Case in point: Jim was a rugged rescue worker who dove into murky waters to retrieve dead bodies. But recently, he developed panic at the thought of driving over the Skyway Bridge, the granddaddy of all local bridges. I told him it is no different than driving anywhere else, because the incline is gradual and almost imperceptible. "You know how to drive straight, don't you?" That was all he needed. The next day I got a call on my voice mail stating only this: "It's Jim. I crossed the bridge easily. I kept telling myself, I know how to drive straight. Thank you for the new mantra."

8. Focus = energy. Let me illustrate: I was petrified to speak in public for the first 25 years of my life. So much so, that in 9th grade speech class I remember praying for Jesus to return to the Earth to end the world before 1:15 Thursday,

when my next speech was due. Today it is my very favorite activity while dressed. How did I overcome the panic and replace it with joy? For one, lots of practice (exposure to the frightening stimulus). For another, I learned to remove the focus from me and put it back on the audience. I would begin a lecture with a question like, "How do you define stress?" Invariably someone in the group would say something funny, the mood would be lightened, and my anxiety was gone. The audience would give flattering reviews, increasing my confidence and thus reducing my anxiety. Today, the bigger the crowd, the better.

9. Breathe/meditate/relax. Practice these tools daily to retrain your brain and nervous system to relax. Ten minutes in the morning can re-route the direction of your entire day.

10. Find an aerobic exercise to implement on a regular basis to reduce panic (and generalized anxiety). Dorothy was a patient of mine with a terrible fear of thunder and lightning, which in southwest Florida, is not unlike living in Manhattan and fearing loud sirens. But Dorothy was open to trying different responses than panic to the storms, a daily occurrence during Florida summers. We decided to try riding the stationary bike at the first hint of rumbling thunder in the distance. Since anxiety is only energy, why not reinvest that energy into something productive, like a good workout? The technique worked so well, Dorothy immediately began to drop some pounds. Moreover, she learned to replace the anxiety and dread with an excitement to jump on her bike and ride.

11. Most importantly, do something. Never wait passively for panic to release you from its grips. Get help. Make a decision to take control of your anxiety.

PANIC BUSTER

A 15-year-old high school student experienced her first panic attack in the hallway of her new high school. There were more than three times the number of students than her last school and she knew exactly two of them. "This is overwhelming!" she told herself, and so, right there, outside science class, she was introduced to panic. Already in therapy for other issues, I ask her to tell me what would happen if she pushed down on the horn of her father's Mustang. "It would blare, of course."

"Even if no one was in the way?"

"Of course."

It will always sound if you push it, regardless of the situation. And you will panic, regardless of the situation, if you think you are trapped or overwhelmed. By the way, there is no crowd of overwhelming kids, just a lot of insecure and frightened high school students, much like you. Tell yourself you belong, be kind to them. Smile a lot, introduce yourself warmly, give out compliments when you think of them. If you think well, you may never panic again.

So far, she hasn't.

Obsessive-Compulsive Disorder (OCD)

There are more things, Lucilius, that frighten us than injure us, and we suffer more in imagination than in reality.

—Seneca

I know you are well aware of obsessive-compulsive disorder (OCD). You describe Uncle Bernie as "So OCD, he makes everyone crazy." You may even apologize to people by saying, "Don't mind me I've been a little OCD since all of my coworkers got sick with the flu last week."

And what do you mean when you say "OCD"? A little rigid, detailed, precautious, controlling, or lacking in spontaneity? It's true, those are characteristics of an obsessive-compulsive personality type, but let me introduce you to the disorder known as OCD.

Obsessions

There are two branches of OCD that the astute reader might guess without prompting: obsessions and compulsions. Let's begin with the former. I'm sure you know what it's like to have a song playing and replaying endlessly in your head, much to your frustration. At a recent kindergarten talent show, no less than nine girls sang the song "Let It Go" from Disney's *Frozen* soundtrack (I would like to compliment both of the girls who sang on key). Gratefully, the children were adorable, but the song remained frozen in the chambers of my mind for the remainder of the day. "Let it go, let it go..." But I just couldn't seem to.

So when you have been diagnosed with OCD, your obsessions are prominent, powerful, and pervasive (and any other P words you can think of). You try but you cannot purge them from your brain. Worse, it's not as benign as a recurrent chorus from a popular song. The obsessive thoughts that comprise a typical OCD patient's mind are threatening or—even more detrimental—terrifying. There is a term in psychiatry/psychology called *ego-dystonic*, which means "not okay with the Self." OCD obsessions are typically ego-dystonic, they are unwanted, unappreciated, and not okay with the Self. Hearing Sunday school songs in your head all day after an hour with second graders is undoubtedly annoying. Believing that your husband's plane will most certainly crash—that's horrifying.

And what do OCD patients typically obsess about? Let me provide you with some real-life examples of obsessions of OCD people:

> "Did I just eat my change?"

> "That white car behind me is gone—did I cause them to crash? Should I turn around and look for them? Are they okay?"

> "I'm going to hurt my family with knives."

> "I won't be able to breathe until October."

> "I can't sit on my car seat; I will become filthy and contaminate my family and pets."

> "Did I just hear that?" (Wondering if others heard what she just did.)

> "Did I lock that door?" (She just checked it 19 times, no exaggeration.)

> "Did that just touch my eye? Is my eye okay?"

The variations are endless, but there are predictable categories where the obsessions seem to manifest themselves: germs/contamination, fear of hurting others, fear-based checking, and contracting illnesses. All of these are unwanted, frightening, and all-consuming to the OCD sufferer.

The suffering is so acute, it is often accompanied by depression, especially due to the feelings of frustration, defeat, and hopelessness experienced by the individual. Although it is very common to combat the obsessions and depressions with medication, especially with anti-depressants and tranquilizers, it is also not unusual for OCD patients to self-medicate with illegal drugs and alcohol. But the most common method to quell the obsessive mind is the creation of a compulsive ritual—a set of predictable, repetitive behaviors—that seem to temporarily satisfy the anxiety.

Compulsions

Richard was never good enough for anything or anyone. His father was critical, his grades were sub average, and he had very few friends to speak of throughout his middle and high school years. In his mind, he was the consummate loser. So when he first experienced symptoms of OCD, Richard was inclined to perceive himself as bad, dirty, and inadequate. Hence, his compulsions took root in a self-grooming/hygiene ritual that dominated his entire morning. It was not unusual for Richard to spend two hours in the shower, 20-plus minutes brushing his teeth, and another 20 combing his hair. Including getting dressed, Richard would sometimes spend as much as three and a half to four hours in the bathroom getting ready. Worse, his wife would sometimes hear him crying in the shower and mumbling, "I'm not clean, I'm not clean enough!"

OCD sufferers seem to have an affected part of the brain known as the *caudate nucleus*. This area of the brain is seemingly more active in the brains of people with OCD. While a normal caudate nucleus (CN) appears to help in detecting errors in your perception of the world, an overly active CN may create the experience that something is wrong and needs to be corrected. Some believe that the rituals are a response to this "something is wrong" mindset. So, essentially, the CN is overly active and creates misperceptions and obsessions in your mind, which lead to repetitive behaviors designed to correct the problem.[1]

Did you know that in some research studies the best treatment for Obsessive Compulsive Disorder (OCD) is being
exposed to the stressor and learning how to respond healthier
to it rather than merely using medication? Learning how to
handle stress in a better way is known as Exposure/Response
Prevention (ERP). Other major studies that looked into
the best treatment options for OCD determined that some
findings suggest that ERP is superior to SRI medication.
Specifically, ERP was associated with larger effect sizes on
OCD measures and fewer residual symptoms compared to
SRIs.[2]

How do we treat OCD?

This may surprise you, but even though OCD is considered to be
primarily a brain disorder, the very best and most successful treatments
are psychological techniques. As we described in Chapter 5, the power
tools of exposure/response preventions (ERP) are considered to be the
treatment of choice.

As described by Dr. Joshua M. Nadeau and Dr. Eric A. Storch, both
of the Department of Pediatrics and the Department of Psychiatry and
Behavioral Neurosciences at the University of South Florida: "Despite
it's impairing nature, there are very effective treatments for individuals with OCD. The most effective single treatment for children and
adults with OCD is cognitive behavioral therapy with exposure and
response prevention. Approximately 85 percent of people benefit from
this approach, which involves the individual gradually and systemati-
cally facing their feared triggers without engaging in associated rituals.
Antidepressant medications are also effective, with about 50-55% of
individuals receiving some benefits."[3]

Let me translate that into the English of non-psychologists: OCD
sufferers are forced to face their fears directly, without resorting to
the familiar comfort of the rituals. That means no re-checking a door
after one lock, washing your hands in the sink once and only once, no

chair-tapping ritual before you leave the room, and absolutely no going back to find out what happened to the white car that disappeared on the highway.

Let's looks at the story of John the Checker (not to be confused with John the Baptist). John was referred to me by his psychiatrist, who had been medicating him for seven years with a combination of anti-depressants and a tranquilizer. He had neither improved nor regressed in the years they had worked together. It was time to try something to enhance the psychological treatment.

John's pattern was a predictable, if not outrageous, ritual of behaviors that made him a spectacle on his quiet cul-de-sac. A bright, astute 37-year-old man, John was aware that the neighborhood children labeled him "the crazy guy."

You see, every morning John would lock his front door and walk to his car parked in the street. John was admittedly frightened of the possibility that a burglar would break into his home and steal all of his hard-earned valuables. Learning that this had, in fact, occurred on the street immediately to the west, John was now hyper-vigilant against this happening to him. In fact, these were the obsessive thoughts that dominated his mindset every time he left his home. It was approximately a 20-second walk to the car. John was amazed at how many catastrophic thoughts he could squeeze into that brief period of time: "They're gonna break into my gun collection, I know it! The guy on the other block never saw it coming—he won't get away with that on me! I hope I locked that front door. I think I did, but...no, I can't risk leaving it unlocked! It'd be like putting a bull's eye on my house. I gotta go back and check, yeah just one time. Okay, I'm going to go back and check."

John would return to the front door, only to find it locked, much to his relief. And this is where the OCD patient differs from the so-called normal individual. The latter tells themselves, "The door is locked for sure, that's good. I can leave for work now." But not so with an OCD patient. He had developed a pattern of behavior that far exceeds what a non-OCD person would do. John repeated the above-mentioned obsessive mindset and, before he could successfully hop into the car and drive away to work, he had worked himself into a lather of anxiety that could be quelled by one thing and one thing only—a return trip to the front door to check the lock! Doing this a second time in less than a minute is pathological for sure, but it never stopped there for John. A third trip up the driveway to repeat this ritual sounds preposterous, but brace yourself, John would re-check his locked door anywhere from 19 to 26 times! It was so debilitating for John that he would leave his house a half-hour before he needed to leave for work. In other words, John knew beforehand that he would engage in this toxic merry-go-round of obsessive thought and ritualistic behavior!

But how and why would he continue with this self-defeating and outrageous behavior? Recall that word *ego-dystonic* mentioned earlier. John's ritualistic walk back and forth from house to car was not humorous to him. In fact, it was a tortuous half hour in which he was at war with himself. He could no more stop at the third or seventh check than a bingeing alcoholic after the first or second drink. He would even climb into the car and, at times, start the car. But he could not take off. He had to check that door!

Behavior is purposeful. There is always a payoff to behavior that is repeated. But where is John's payoff? He already knows the door is locked. Or does he? John only knows for sure that he feels horribly anxious when he attempts to take off to work. Rechecking the door calms that anxiety, if only momentarily, more than anything else in the world, short of having armed guards patrolling his door day and night.

So why 26 times? How is that better than two, nine, or 17? And why would Richard (mentioned earlier in this chapter) require a two-hour shower instead of 12 or 37 minutes?

From the best of my understanding, the repetition of these behaviors serves to reduce the sufferer's anxiety, bit by bit. There is no magic in the number of minutes (unless the number is the compulsion itself, a need to do something four times, for instance, to ensure that no harm befalls any of their three kids). The reason the repetition seems to work is because it erodes the anxiety and exhausts the individual through the excessive number of repetitions. In other words, it is hard to maintain that high level of anxiety for an extended period of time due to the sheer exhaustion (this is also why people are encouraged to face their fears for prolonged periods of time in a technique called *flooding*).

So after half an hour, John's anxiety is significantly less because it (and he) is now exhausted by his rituals. This is stored in his brain as a successful event and that the ritual behaviors worked to cure his anxiety. And, as we all know, whatever behavior works will be repeated. John will resume his rituals once again tomorrow morning. Why? Because they feel like they work.

So how did I finally help John champion his OCD ritual? We began with making a "baseline" of how many times John re-checked his door in the course of a week. He had days of 20 and 25, for instance, and ended up averaging approximately 22 times per morning. He kept this daily log in a journal, wherein he recorded the date and time, as well as the re-check totals.

We then began to rehearse a reality-based self-talk (recall the talking back to Self tool in Chapter 4). How often do you get robbed, John? What is the base rate of breaking and entering? Of course, the answer was zero and only once in the 17 years he had lived in his neighborhood had anyone been robbed. But, John's pattern of checking and re-checking was now associated with the success he enjoyed of zero break-ins to his house. To John's way of thought, his re-checking was not only responsible for reducing his anxiety but also preventing the burglars from invading his home.

Of course, two things that occur together are not necessarily linked together. (Try telling that to a sports fan whose team came from behind to win the game, only after he turned his hat backward.) But on a neurological level, John was convinced that his pattern of incessant re-checking prevented the burglaries.

Back to John's journal. I asked him to begin to consider the reality that his behavior of re-checking was completely un-connected from the burglaries. That was the only assignment for week two: process the new thinking while he walked to and from the car. As a result, he reduced his week two total to an average of 18 times, nowhere near a cure, but a statistically significant difference from week one. Cognitively, he now had the means to understand his behavior and challenge his faulty belief that his ritual was indeed a successful deterrent for thieves. His average weekly total dropped again in week three to 15 and then to 10 in week four. By the end of the fifth week, John's re-checking number was down to five times, a very significant decrease from his presenting baseline.

At this point, John was able to articulate another important reality—a good thief could probably gain access to his house despite a locked door. That is, he could cut screens, break windows, and even climb down the chimneys like Bad Santa, he quipped. So at this point we elected to introduce response prevention with a dose of positive reinforcement. John was asked to state aloud, "I am now locking my door. It is locked!" Next he was asked to sprint to his car, unlock the door, start the car, and drive away before he could reconsider. John liked the challenge; he used a creative image from his childhood days and ran as if enemy snipers were shooting him. He would drive away from the danger before they could hit him.

Just in case that challenge wasn't enough, I introduced a special reward for John to consider. He was a big Tampa Bay Lightning hockey fan and would love nothing more than a ticket to a home game. I knew that we could get John's wife on board to justify the expenditure for a ticket in exchange for two straight weeks of zero checking. One phone call later, she was a teammate on our plan.

The combination of rational thinking, response prevention, talking back to himself, mindfulness (staying in the here and now), and then shifting his focus to a childhood fantasy (focus = energy), in addition to positive reinforcement, somehow added up to a successful outcome for John. He earned the right to a Lightning game and never looked back.

He no longer checks his front door after locking it once. However, there was one remaining problem: the neighbors still thought he was "the crazy guy" for ducking imaginary bullets on his morning run to the car, but he reported this with a victorious smile.

Take Home Messages:

1. Obsessions are intrusive thoughts or feelings that are unwanted and persistent.

2. Compulsions are repetitive behaviors that are performed to quiet the uncomfortable feelings caused by the obsessions or to prevent something bad from happening. Remember the compulsion provides only short-term relief.

3. The single most effective treatment of OCD is Cognitive Behavioral Therapy with Exposure and Response Prevention.

4. Since you have taught yourself to use the repetitive/compulsive behavior to cope with your intrusive thoughts or feelings you can unlearn this association and develop healthier coping skills that provide long-term benefits.

5. Each time you use a garden or power tool instead of your compulsion you are rewiring your brain for a healthier future.

Exercises
1. What is my OCD cycle?
A. List the triggers in your life that lead to your compulsive behaviors.
B. List your thoughts or feelings that are unpleasant that usually lead to the compulsive behaviors.
C. List the repetitive or compulsive behaviors that you turn to in an attempt to quiet your thoughts or feelings, or to prevent something from happening.

Exercises (continued)

2. Practicing to use a new cycle.

A. List your repetitive behaviors that provide short-term relief.

B. List healthier options from the garden or power tools that you will use as positive alternatives to your intrusive thoughts and feelings.

C. Describe the potential benefits of using these tools instead of your compulsion.

Exercises (continued)
3. Stopping your OCD cycle.
A. List the healthier garden or power tools you will use to cope with your stress.
B. Describe the benefits of using the above coping skills tools on your intrusive thoughts or feelings.
C. Remember: the more you practice or rehearse using these tools, the more skilled you are when you need to use them. Describe the benefits of using the coping skills after each trigger.

9 Generalized Anxiety Disorder (GAD)

*Worry never robs tomorrow of its sorrow, it only
saps today of its joys.*

—Leo Buscaglia

Dr. Christina was just like you and me, except she could afford a 14-night cruise in the Mediterranean with her husband. Perfect spring weather, five-star accommodations, his and her massages. Absolute perfection.

So why was she *looking* for something to worry about?

> Did you know that new research has discovered why and how traumatic memories seem to become so well established in our memory? When exposed to a negative experience, the brain releases two chemicals, cortisol and norepinephrine, which strengthen memories. So, if we can learn how to better respond after a traumatic event, we can lower the levels of these two chemicals and prevent this memory enhancing process.[1]

Chances are, you may know a Christina or, possibly, you *personally* relate to her plight. Everything is going okay; there is nothing to complain about other than your weight is up and your profits are down. Nothing desperate. And yet if you are awake, there you are, worrying your pretty little head about something or other. Rest/relaxation is difficult, because you sabotage it at the first opportunity. Why? Because to relax is tantamount to letting your guard down and becoming vulnerable to whatever grenades life might toss at you. There is always something, and it's never easy. If it isn't one thing, it's two things. So you've learned the hard way to scan the horizon for any potential threat, from your teenage daughter's rebellious piercings to your father's failing kidneys—how can you *ever* find a moment of true peace? You can't seem to gain meaningful communication with your husband, your workouts aren't keeping you as fit as you used to be, and life seems to have stomped all over your face with its crow's feet. Is it any wonder you have turned to chardonnay (chardon-b and chardon-c)?

Don't look now, but you may be suffering from a diagnosis of generalized anxiety disorder (GAD). You certainly aren't alone; more than three out of 100 people may be diagnosed as such, with the average age of onset being just over 30.

Understanding GAD

Unlike some other psychiatric disorders, generalized anxiety disorder appears aptly named. The symptoms are indeed generalized, that is, they occur even in the absence of specific stressors. Your anxiety is the norm; it is not about your doctor's appointment, SAT exam, or special assessment from the condo association. You are anxious because you are alive, and sometimes, your anxiety is how you know you're still alive. It greets you in the morning before you even get up and out of bed, and reminds you of its presence when you hit the pillow at night. In fact, to qualify for the GAD diagnosis, you have suffered with unrelenting anxiety symptoms for at least six months; you try, but you can't seem to find the valve that shuts it down. It literally feels as if it is outside of your control. Likewise, the anxiety feels bigger than any situation you are battling. That's because it is. It's not about today's struggles, it's about the way you are perceiving reality: your life is one huge, inescapable barrage of threatening experiences, or, as my favorite octogenarian neighbor puts it: "Life is one big pain in the ass, ain't it Doc?"

The GAD sufferer experiences today as a series of threats to withstand and tomorrow's forecast is for doom and gloom, with a chance of things getting worse. To quote an old Paul Simon song, "A good day ain't got no rain. A bad day's when you lay in bed and think of things that might have been."

It's not like Panic Disorder in that there are no sudden "attacks" of anxiety. It's different than OCD in that you are not plagued with a need to scrub your hands until your fingerprints come off. It's unlike PTSD, because you are not overwhelmed by a horrible scene from your past that you just can't seem to get over. It's not like a phobia where all you need to do is avoid one scary thing and you're fine. GAD is an everyday, all the time, in your face, "I feel so nervous, unsettled, and vulnerable in my own skin that I want to scream" disorder.

> Did you know that in 2013 the Canadian Psychological Association reviewed the best practice treatments for anxiety disorder? They identified some great research from the National Institute for Health and Care Excellence (NICE), which recommended Cognitive Behavior Therapy as a first-line treatment for Generalized Anxiety Disorder (GAD).[2]

Just in case you require a deeper understanding check out these symptoms that are all associated with GAD: you are drained and exhausted from the chronic worry; your muscles are tense; your sleep onset may be delayed by your inability to relax; likewise, your sleep cycle may be compromised, resulting in more fatigue; you may be restless and irritable. Dysphoria (low mood) is likely because you can't seem to gain relief; substance abuse is certainly an option because it's a way to get that relief, albeit temporarily.

Additionally, anxiety may manifest itself in real physical problems from headaches to heart attacks. This is called somatization: turning psycho-emotional struggles into physical situations and even chronic illnesses and disease. Gastrointestinal issues are often the first place anxiety appears in children, and chronic anxiety may result in diarrhea, constipation, or even contribute to the exacerbation of Crohn's disease or diverticulitis.

Causes of GAD

Like virtually all human illnesses and diagnoses, there seems to be a genetic component to GAD. You may be predisposed to symptoms of GAD if it is in your DNA. But always remember capacity does not equal destiny. You are not predetermined to suffer from GAD just because your Aunt Bertha worried from dawn to dusk, or cousin Paul converted anxiety into a compulsive counting of rosary beads. It is you who will determine if you suffer from GAD.

Remember: it is your thinking patterns—perceiving the world as a dangerous place, expecting people to hurt you, or things to never work out—that creates the foundation for GAD.

But don't early experiences contribute? Of course they do. Growing up in a family that was riddled by alcoholism, violence, divorce, infidelity, verbal conflicts, financial worries, homelessness, prolonged unemployment, and so on, all contribute to the possibility that you may someday be diagnosed with GAD. Think of it this way: if you grow up in or near a battle zone, it wouldn't be surprising if you geared up for battle even after the war was long over. GAD is your way of never, ever letting your guard down just because of the possibility that something bad might happen. And every time it does, that serves as proof-positive that you must never make the mistake of dropping your guard again.

> A recent study revealed that the use of Facebook predicted a decline in your adult sense of well-being. The researchers assessed: 1) how people feel moment-to-moment and 2) how satisfied they are with their lives. The use of Facebook predicted a negative shift on both factors. Though Facebook provides an invaluable resource to so many people around the world and offers an opportunity for social connections, this research shows how people make negative comparisons of themselves to what they see posted online. Here's an idea: try posting this research article.[3]

Whatever you practice, you will increase your proficiency. That includes speaking Portuguese, riding a unicycle, or trimming your handlebar mustache. You can actually train yourself to think like a worrisome person which, in turn, trains your nervous system to respond in fight or flight mode—the stress response—even though you are in no life-threatening danger. Push the threat button often enough, and you maintain that guarded high stress posture as the norm.

You actually navigate your life in stress mode, just as if you were walking alone at night in a bad neighborhood. But don't blame your nervous system, because it is taking direct orders from you (your mind). You instruct yourself to stay aroused (anxious) by thinking and re-thinking the same thoughts of threat, danger, betrayal, financial ruin, failure, rejection, and male pattern baldness. Think those thoughts once and you create anxiety. Think them a lot and you become adept at thinking them and staying anxious. Think them even more and you *train your nervous system to operate in a chronic state of stress and anxiety!* And, that, my nervous friend, is how you became the subject of this chapter on GAD.

> In a 2007 study of 7,076 individuals in the Netherlands, the research indicated that anxiety disorders preceded the onset of alcohol dependence.[4]

Dr. Christina's Story

Let's return to the promenade deck of the cruise ship where Dr. Christina is probably sunburned by now. Before we explore her successful treatment, please take a moment to read her story, written in her words:

> *Sometimes I think I have been anxious my whole life, starting before I was born, while I was still in my mother's womb. To try and imagine that I felt unsafe even there seems unbelievable but true. Luckily my own nature was calm, otherwise I would be a completely jittery person. Instead, I feel a sense of inner peacefulness surrounded by chaos and fear.*

My mother was a Japanese concentration camp survivor. She spent her 16th, 17th, and 18th birthdays in Santo Tomas, a Japanese concentration camp in the Philippines. Although she survived, she was left with emotional, physical, and spiritual scars which she passed on to her five children. Until her ultimate suicide, she remained fearful of starving to death or of being bombed.

She gave birth to me about nine years after Santo Tomas while she was again "interned," although this time in a mental hospital. When I was a baby, she always kept me near, because she said I was such a joyful, peaceful baby and because she was afraid of losing me. As a child, I felt responsible for her moods and for her well-being. I'd even accompany her to her psychiatrist visits where she was medicated with Dexedrine to quell her fears of starving and meprobamate to help her sleep and hold back her fears of being bombed. My father died unexpectedly when I was 10, leaving me not only the responsibility of my mother, but also my brothers and sisters. Throughout my childhood, whenever I showed my independence and lack of devotion to her every need, she would throw a temper tantrum, which would usually end when she took an overdose of medication (often begging me to give her the pills) and then fell asleep or became sedated enough for me to drag her to a mental hospital.

In therapy I realized I have lived my 62 years in a state of anxiety and that, in so many ways, I had not fully lived my life because my anxiety did not permit me to appreciate fully any moment of my life. I had been addicted to anxiety, which colored everything I did, saw, or felt. And unfortunately, I had passed this overwhelming sense of anxiety to my son.

I realized that although I could not do anything to change the past or relive my past, I could not make up for the terrible inheritance I had given my son. However, I could somehow rid myself of this old anxiety—and then I could reassure my son and give him the peace he had always needed.

The realization that I had missed/lost most of my life to anxiety made me cry. I cried for the loss of so much beauty and fulfillment and just plain living that had passed me by while I just stood there worrying about who knows what.

One day after an amazing massage while on a cruise in the Mediterranean, I tried to relax but my mind kept searching for something to worry about...and that day, I couldn't find anything to worry about. *Although this made me laugh, it was a stark picture of my addiction to worry. I was going through withdrawal.*

The feeling of worry is very complicated for me—it contains a sense of powerlessness, an inability to change the inevitable gloom of the world. It also contains a feeling of hopelessness and of anger. I have to admit that I have felt and continue to feel angry at the people who have made me feel anxious, angry that they have not done their part to keep things together. And although I can and do forgive them for this, I know they will continue to let me down. Their past failures, although I understand and forgive, have become what I expect from them.

As a child, I felt that the inevitable was my mother's insane angry tantrums, which I could not stop or avoid, no matter how good I was. As an adult the inevitable was always expected: my world would fall apart. Although I might appear confident and in control, I was really standing/crouching at the brink of a huge disaster about to happen... and I was always ready to keep things from falling apart, in my own life or in anyone else's.

It is hard for me to sit back, especially if everything is not perfect, because I get anxious. And even when things are perfect, I look around wondering when the next shoe will fall. I'm trying now to unaddict myself from this need for anxiety. Anxiety is a motivating force for me. It helps me see what's wrong and what needs to be fixed. It gives me the energy to fix things, to keep moving toward the positive, to not be content with the present. What will motivate me if I don't have this anxiety and sense of urgency?

I have to find another source of energy that comes from deep within me, from my sense of inner peace, which is hard to find. I have to tell myself that I do have some control in every situation although it may not appear that way...and that I can trust the people I love, including my son and my husband, to do the right thing. I have to have the wisdom to accept what I can and cannot do to make things better—and to have the faith in others to do what they need to do—and to know that it never helps make anything better when I stick my hands into the mess. I have to just take a step back and breathe and wait until a path clears and I can see it. I have the ability to encourage myself and my husband and son, especially if I show my respect for myself, my husband, my son, and my friends and family, when I stand back and let each do his or her part—and encourage that by saying positive things or expressing my belief in each of our ability to grow or change

*and become more focused, competent, and alive...and less anxious
or worried about bad outcomes, believing in each of us being able to
do the right thing.*

> Suffering from an anxiety disorder puts you in a very high-
> risk category for also suffering a mood disorder, like major
> depression. Depending upon which study you read, depres-
> sion "co-occurs" with anxiety disorders anywhere from 37
> percent to well over 70 percent of the time. One thing is clear:
> people who are anxious are very often depressed and vice
> versa. No word on which is chicken and which is egg.[5]

The good doctor, as far as she could remember, was always the
one fixing things. A mentally ill mother and a hardworking father
for Christina meant that she would be assuming the role of family
caregiver. Her mother's illness would surface in explosive and disruptive episodes and then, just as quickly, disappear into periods of normalcy again. Christina responded initially by feeling wounded by her
mom's explosions, and personalizing the fact that she was often the
target. She would also retreat into denial, as survivors of domestic
abuse often do, minimizing the impact of the rages upon her. Instead
of allowing herself to be angry about the mistreatment, she found it
safer to deny the episodes and become anxious and guarded about
doing anything to trigger another explosive incident. She became convinced that she must be doing something to trigger this ugliness in her
mother's behavior and, therefore, it was up to her to figure out how to
prevent its reoccurrence.

As you've already read in Christina's story, her father died suddenly,
her mother grew sicker, and Christina became caregiver for her mother
and all four of her younger siblings. Feelings of hurt, anger, or even
the fear or being overwhelmed were luxuries that Christina could not
afford at that time. Every emotion that she experienced was funneled
into a familiar disturbance, gnawing in the pit of her stomach. That

ever-present anxiety, paradoxically, was her one source of comfort and companionship, and at the same time, sucked the joy out of each and every moment of her life.

> Did you know that a significant amount of emergency room visits are due to anxiety, depression or substance abuse problems? In 2007, the Agency for Healthcare Research and Quality (AHRQ) found that almost one in eight of the 95 million visits to emergency departments in the United States were due to mental health and/or substance abuse problems. The most common reason for these visits was a mood disorder (42.7 percent), followed by anxiety disorders (26.1%), alcohol-related problems (22.9 percent) and drug disorders (17.6 percent).[6]

To experience joy is to be in the moment, mindful. For Christina, that mindfulness was far too dangerous, as she risked a painful outcome of some sort—her mom exploding, or worse yet, attempting suicide. So she guarded herself with a protective coating of worry, one that she carried into her adult years. Interestingly, her worry manifested as a controlling, if not suffocating, blanket thrown on top of her husband and her son, in an effort to weather-proof them from all potential sources of harm. And, as you might imagine, whenever either of them veered off the chosen path and dangerously close to the rocks—her husband once had an affair and her son's career was never launched—Christina engaged in two familiar behaviors: 1) blaming herself for not preventing the bad outcome (she should have seen the affair coming, and therefore could have somehow averted it), and/or 2) working even harder at scanning her world for potential threats and dangers to ward them off by controlling others with advice, instruction, and, of course, worry.

Treating GAD

So how did we succeed in treating Christina's GAD? It was vital for Christina to tell her story—get her stuff off the floor, so to speak (see Chapter 4). She needed to express and finally release some long-standing pain, sadness, sorrow, and eventually anger and resentment. These were toxic emotions that fueled Christina's anxiety and protective worry. She worked hard at understanding the purpose(s) of her worry and how it seemed to work for her when really, it became a negative addiction that robbed her of joy.

Christina needed to learn to let go of worry and replace it with faith, especially in the two people she worried about the most, her son and her husband, respectively. As a life-long caregiver, Christina learned that people would not fare well without her nurturance and support. It was time to let go of her need to control her son and risk that he would crash and burn without her omnipresent guidance. But a funny thing happened; her son prospered when instead of advising, controlling, and fretting over him on the phone, she encouraged him by telling him she knew he could do it. He confessed that he saw her worrisome behaviors as insults to him and his capabilities. Whenever Christina would show her emotional upset, he concluded that his own mother believed he was incompetent, so how could he believe in himself?

> Did you know that a study of elderly patients with dementia who were cared for in a psychiatric center with animal-assisted therapy demonstrated lower levels of anxiety, phobias, and aggression than those matched in every way except the use of animal-assisted therapy sessions?[7]

On the homefront, the devastation that followed Christina's learning of her husband's affair produced an immediate need to control his whereabouts—that's a no-brainer. But the childhood message to control and nurture others or risk losing them was also prominent for Christina. Obviously, she disappointed her husband somehow; his affair was proof that she was, in fact, a failure. If she were as perfect as she strived to be, this would not happen. It could not happen.

Christina was surprised to learn that her husband shared in her devastation, and that he, too, experienced the affair as being the worst thing he had ever been through. He recognized that what he really wanted was a better connection with the one woman that he loved. His brokenness convinced her that she needed to invest her energies in appreciating and loving him, not smothering him with her anxiety and desperation.

Once again, the message was clear: for Christina to achieve any degree of peace and happiness, she needed to let go of control, not increase the intensity of her worry and micro-management of others. That is, replace the worry with faith in herself. Also, that she could be happy even if her world was wrought with problems. It was time to trust that she could be well even if her life was not picture perfect.

Christina surprised herself with the realization that even though she was a high-functioning and unquestionably competent physician, she held on to a secret addiction, much like many of her patients. Only in her case, it was not alcohol, cocaine, gambling, or porn that dominated her waking hours. It was worry.

Addiction to Worry

Worry? Can you really become *addicted* to an activity like worry? The simple answer is yes. You can become addicted to fluffernutter sandwiches, if that's your thing. If you consider that addiction is characterized essentially by changes in your brain's neurochemistry, that without your substance/activity you will experience certain withdrawal symptoms (irritability, depression, or anxiety, for example).

A second characteristic of addiction is known as increased tolerance, wherein you require at least as much of your substance/activity, if not more, to achieve the desired result. If you, like so many athletes, require a pre-game ritual (say stretching, for instance) that becomes necessary before a game, less stretching time is not the norm. You will need to maintain at least that ritual or perhaps increase it to avoid withdrawal symptoms. Likewise, if two oxycodone pills are needed to launch you to your private nirvana, addiction means that nothing less than this amount will suffice. Over time, you may even require more.

Christina needed to worry, because without this activity, she became edgy, nervous, and irritable, as if experiencing a nicotine withdrawal. So worry and only worry could provide the equivalent of a Marlboro, settling her body down by flooding her mind with thoughts of catastrophic outcomes.

Sounds crazy, doesn't it? But again, you can become addicted to anything that provides you with a desired feeling or outcome. The desired outcome was the perception of control, which Christina, like any professional worrier, became addicted to and yearned for whenever things in her life got a little dicey, especially regarding her husband or son.

So Christina and I resorted to many cognitive-based activities, designed to change her emotions by changing her thinking. We employed garden tools like "What is the worst that could happen?" "If he is unfaithful again, I will deal with it appropriately." (We also replaced worry with faith in Self.) The focus = energy principle was an important tool to encourage Christina to spend her days in a positive place and to steer away from self-destructive thinking. She was encouraged to replace catastrophic worrying about her son with simple, encouraging text messages like "Thinking of you—I'm so proud of you! xo Mom."

We also employed cognitive restructuring, replacing negative thoughts with realistic and positive thoughts, such as "My work is such a blessing; I adore my son; my marriage is better than ever; I can release my caregiver role now as an adult."

Christina was reminded to embrace the healthiest person in the world concept—as far as I was concerned, she wasn't far away from being that person, as long as she wasn't torturing herself with worry. As a healthy, confident physician, she could think the following: whatever happens in life, "I have the skills to handle it. In the meantime, I will enjoy my day!" (Obviously, this incorporates mindfulness thinking, as well.)

She also learned to employ the garden tools of making plans and utilizing communication skills and boundaries because, as we rehearsed in the serenity prayer tool, Christina needed to take control over what was hers to control. She let her husband know that she would choose to trust him once more, but if he were unfaithful again she would certainly divorce him. (An important communication/boundary.)

But cognitive exercises and changes in thinking, however important, are but one of the two types of interventions that Christina and I utilized in her recovery. (Recall that the three ways to alter emotion include biochemical, sensorimotor, and cognitive.) We also employed an all-out sensorimotor assault on her anxiety: Christina was a swimmer, the type of athlete who could traverse an Olympic-sized pool for 90 consecutive minutes without requiring an oxygen tank. She became cognizant of the notion that anxiety was an energy she could convert into jet-fuel for her aquatic workouts, the ultimate lemon into lemonade.

Moreover, she was more than willing to re-train her nervous system with her own brand of spirituality/relaxation: yoga. Christina found that she could combine her new cognitions with her yoga exercises and meditation with the mantra: "I trust God's will in my life."

Ultimately, the threats that Christina had been so invested in throughout the years were proving to be far less threatening and, as such, her anxiety symptoms were waning right before her eyes. This, in turn, served to increase her confidence, which put her in a place where she no longer required worry to keep her catastrophes away, because she no longer needed to create catastrophes in the first place. She could let her mind be quiet. And that quiet, instead of leaving her mind with a need to overwhelm herself with the noise and clutter of life's potential horrors, was now an acceptable option for Christina. She even learned to enjoy the peace and quiet.

So there, on the sun-drenched cruise ship on the Mediterranean, Christina spoke back to herself confidently, saying only, "All is quiet. There is no fear. All is good. I trust God's will in my life."

Take Home Messages:

1. GAD isn't full of ups and downs or particularly terrifying moments. It is experienced as more of a relentless feeling that something bad is about to happen.

2. The resulting difficulties that are associated with GAD will leave you feeling like Eeyore looks. Poor donkey, kind of sad, fatigued, and unable to really enjoy much of anything— all of the time.

3. Practice contributes to the development of GAD and it will be awareness and practice that will eliminate it.

4. We can become addicted to anything that alters the way we feel in a positive way—including worrying. Remember what is reinforced is repeated. What we feed, grows.

5. Learning, practicing, and establishing boundaries is vital. YOU are the only thing truly within your control.

Exercises

1. Take a few moments to sit quietly and reflect on the parts of your life you enjoy. Then, using five pages of paper, write one of your favorite moments of your life at the top of each page. Reflecting on that favorite moment, write down what it was that you liked about it. What did it represent? Did it signify something in particular? Once you have your thoughts about why each of those moments is a favorite, go back to each page and list the personal qualities you have that contributed to each of those favorite moments.

2. Using the pages from Exercise 1, make a single list of the qualities from each page. Do you find one quality or characteristic appearing several times? Once you have all of the qualities listed on a sheet, you will likely find two or three (or 10 or 11) that were listed more than once. Write these on a card to carry with you or note it in your phone or write it on your washroom mirror in lipstick. Do whatever you have to do to remind yourself of those qualities that you possess that have brought about the best moments of your life. Then, using the note as a reminder, mindfully use as many of those qualities every day for a week and discover what power you have over the outcomes of your life!

3. Learn the first verse of the Serenity Prayer and then practice living it every day:

Serenity Prayer

God grant me the serenity

to accept the things I cannot change;

courage to change the things I can;

and wisdom to know the difference.

10 Post-Traumatic Stress Disorder (PTSD)

If you are going through hell, keep going.

—Winston Churchill

There are too few instances in life to talk—let alone write—about the middle toe on my right foot. From all indications, it is an oft-neglected part of one's anatomy. So I'm hoping this is one such opportunity.

One afternoon at the office, my patient failed to show up for an appointment, so I had a free hour to myself. The top of the middle toe on my right foot had been sore to the touch for several months, so I decided to shred my shoe and sock to investigate. The top of the toe was layered with excess skin, unlike any of the other toes. Looking below the skin, I saw a black dot embedded deeply into the toe. I decided to scratch at the layers of skin and remove the excess from the toe, in an effort to gain access to the black dot. I squeezed the toe only to reveal a small amount of liquid puss encasing a half-inch long wood splinter. Upon the removal of the splinter, the excess skin did not grow back and the toe never hurt again.

And then it occurred to me—my middle toe story is a perfect metaphor for post-traumatic stress disorder. Let's explore the metaphor further: my toe, unbeknownst to me, was traumatized by a very intrusive splinter. The splinter is invasive and does not belong within the toe; it needs to be expelled. But the owner/operator of the toe is oblivious to the intruder and only remotely connected to the pain. As such, the intrusive splinter remains. Since the splinter is not being removed, the body finds it necessary to protect the toe from further attacks and sensitivity to the pain by providing the protective coating of excess skin. In this way, the toe (and the surrounding foot) is still quite functional despite the now buried and well-protected splinter. And yet, because something is wrong, there is pain and discomfort. Perhaps someone should call a toe truck. (Sorry, I couldn't resist.)

So, what does this have to do with post-traumatic stress disorder (PTSD)? According to the *Diagnostic and Statistical Manual of the American Psychological Association*, PTSD is defined as the "development of characteristic symptoms following exposure to one or more dramatic events."[1]

Essentially, this is the progression of PTSD. Something perceived as traumatic happens to you. It could be a fire, rape, combat, tornado, an auto accident, and so on. You survive the trauma, but are aware at some point that life doesn't feel the same as it did prior to the trauma. There are a number of issues/symptoms that are present that were not a part of your life before you were traumatized.

Let's take a look at these symptoms in three major clusters (and revisit my middle toe):

Cluster #1: Re-experiencing the trauma

As we learned in Chapter 4, the human mind likes to finish things; from projects to conversations, to books on anxiety, we seek closure. To leave things unfinished, undigested, as it were, is to give them the power to return. I like to tell people that the mind is like the stomach: whatever hasn't been digested can repeat on you. There is, however, a major difference: the stomach can only keep food undigested for approximately 12 hours. You will not re-experience a peanut butter and jelly sandwich consumed in the third grade, but you might replay the traumatic beating you watched your mother absorb that evening. The mind can keep something undigested (unresolved) for 60, 70, even 80 years later. Often times, traumatic material is repressed, or occluded from conscious memory, only to be remembered partially or completely decades later. Sometimes this is because it is stimulated by something similar to your experiences. For instance, you may become anxious and unusually protective of your 9-year old daughter before you even remember that you were molested at that age. (For a more detailed discussion on such, see the Bibliography for additional sources).

Did you know that the U.S. Department of Veterans Affairs (2013, www.ptsd.va.gov/public) published a booklet that was produced by the National Center for PTSD? They recommended three forms of treatment. The first treatment listed was Psychotherapy, specifically Cognitive-Behavioral Therapy (CBT), which was identified as the "most effective treatment for PTSD as well as the two most researched types of CBT: Cognitive Processing Therapy (CPT) and Prolonged Exposure (PE). As an alternative to prolonged exposure, check out my 5-step healing technique later in this chapter.[2]

There are certain predictable symptoms of the first cluster of PTSD (re-experiencing the trauma): intrusive reconnections of the event; flashbacks of the trauma; nightmares about the trauma.

Nancy was 55 years old when she began to experience intrusive and frightening images of her long-since deceased grandfather chasing her around his dining room table. She didn't know any more than that at the time, nor was she sure that she wanted to know anymore. It was very frightening and unsettling to Nancy. She knew which age this experience took place—she was left with her grandparents for a summer when she was 6 years old. But she didn't know what she would remember next.

Merely by poking at the memory of the chasing grandfather, asking simple non-leading questions (What is happening? Where are you? Are you alone or with others?), Nancy re-experienced terrifying memories of his visiting and molesting her in the attic of his home, where she slept. She could extract many specific details from her memory, all of which were buried and inaccessible to her before the flashes of the table chase. She could smell his pipe tobacco breath up close; feel his cold, hard fingers painfully penetrating her vagina; and even hear her grand-mother's voice calling up after him; "John are you up there bothering that child again? Jesus!"

With the voicing of Nancy's memories came the accompanying and appropriate emotional expression. She whimpered, cried, held her breath, hid under my afghan, crossed her legs, and even yelled once at her perpetrating grandfather. She reported somatic (body) symptoms of pain and blood in her underwear upon awakening one morning. Interestingly, but not surprisingly, the pain and the bleeding corre-sponded with the expressing and release of her memory. She "recov-ered" five instances in all, each one painful and humiliating to her, as well as extremely frightening, but none involving intercourse. She remembered an attempt on his part to encourage fellatio, but it ended awkwardly with her choking and coughing amidst his frustration. On the fifth and final memory, Nancy began to sob when her grandfather arrived and pulled back her covers. He seemingly evaluated her reac-tion and decided it wasn't worth it to pursue anymore. "Okay," he said. He walked away, climbed down the attic stairs, and never bothered her again.

Nancy recovered completely from all aspects of the grandfather's molestations, but it required her to work through each of the memories as they emerged by expressing and releasing the concomitant emotional pain. She has never needed to return to the attic again, because, as she relates, "that is all over and done."

The flashbacks, the re-experiencing of the trauma through the body memories (blood and vaginal pain), the smells and sensations, were all indications that something wasn't finished for Nancy. It held power over her once until it was completed—remembered, felt, expressed, and released. And then it was finished. Done. Completed. For good.

Back to the toe: the symptoms of pain and sensitivity to touch are again, analogous to that first cluster of PTSD, re-experiencing the event. How? The pain, like the flashes and fear of the chase with Grandpa, call attention to the fact that the trauma isn't finished. There is still something wrong—there is a bleepin' splinter embedded in my toe!

Pain, as we all know, is a sign that something is amiss in the system—so are flashbacks, recurrent nightmares, and obsessing on decades of old memories. If any of this is happening to you, it is time to slay the dragon (see Chapter 4) and remove the splinter!

Cluster #2: Avoidance of the trauma

The second cluster of PTSD is *avoidance*, the Darth Vader of "A" words (again, see Chapter 4). You probably know veterans who won't go near crowded theme parks or 4th of July celebrations, because it reminds them too much of their personal horrors of combat. Each exploding firework sends their anxiety level skyrocketing out of control.

Avoidance of trauma occurs in so many ways: Dale wouldn't drive anywhere near the part of town where he was molested by the clergy person at his house of worship; Claudia was "freaked out" by all men with beards after being held up at gun point by a bearded man.

And then there was Clara, a woman in her mid-50s who was being treated for relationship issues and a need to find more fulfillment in her life. One day Clara mentioned casually that she and her husband were looking for a new place to live and may have found the perfect house, but it was in a wooded area and that wasn't going to work. "What is the problem with living near the woods?" I asked, because that is what psychologists do. She didn't know, but she knew that there was a problem with the woods and she would get to the bottom of it next session.

Clara appeared promptly and well dressed for the next session as usual. She told me she was ready and asked if I minded if she lay down on the couch. She closed her eyes and without a word from me, immersed herself in what appeared to be a hypnotic trance. What happened next was, to me, unforgettable: she related a story about vacationing with her parents (she was about 7) in a wooded campground, taking a walk away from camp, and hearing the angry exchange of voices. Clara reportedly hid behind a tree and watched a tattooed man with a dirty blue bandana repeatedly strike another man with what appeared to be a stone, until he lay motionless, bleeding in a small brook, presumably murdered.

Clara shook, bounced up and down on the couch, and at times cried hysterically at the telling of her story. I said nary a word. By the end of the session she was greatly relieved by the expression and release of her childhood trauma. She was amazed at the realization that she had carried that horrible incident silently, unbeknownst to her for a half a century. The only awareness Clara had was a nagging anxiety whenever she was out in nature; she also had a need to avoid wooded areas. Predictably, she also had an aversion to men with bandanas and tattoos.

At the American Psychological Association 2014 Annual Convention in Washington, D.C., some important and surprising results from a congressionally mandated study funded by the U.S. Department of Veterans Affairs were revealed. Based on data collected from 2,348 participants enrolled in the National Vietnam Veterans Longitudinal Study (1986–1988), this study was performed as a 25-year follow up to the original 1980s research. They found that veterans who had developed PTSD from war zone stress died at a rate of 2:1 compared to those veterans without PTSD. As quoted in Medscape Medical News, William Schlenger, PhD, the principal scientist, said, "So the finding that there are almost 300,000 Vietnam veterans who have PTSD today 4 decades after they left the battlefield is a very important finding, and it lets us know what's likely going to happen in the folks who have come home from Iraq and Afghanistan. The study's key take-away is that for many veterans with PTSD, the war is not over."[3]

My middle toe also had a way to promote avoidance, the second cluster of PTSD. How? The excess skin, the body's layer of protection, kept a layered coating around the splinter to ward off any other potential threats to the toe. Ironically, avoidance, like the excess skin, also works *against* the healing process. If Clara could not repress her horrible memory, she would have been forced to address it much earlier in her life. Likewise, the excess skin served to minimize my pain and discomfort, so the toe was left unaddressed for months. If the pain were acute and severe, needless to say, it would have inspired a call for action much more immediately.

Cluster #3: Increased Arousal

The third cluster of PTSD is known as a "heightened sense of arousal." Simply put, the mind is operating like an armed guard, protecting valuable assets or people. Think of the guys at Fort Knox looking for anyone or anything suspicious that might threaten the valuables inside the fort. The symptoms of the third cluster include: extreme anxiety, hyper-vigilance (overly watchful or suspicious), exaggerated startle response (walking in a room unannounced might send someone into a rage or panic response), and emotional anesthesia (feeling numb or dead inside).

Remember the story of Marsha, the woman who was abducted from the park at gunpoint? (See Chapter 4.) She decided, consciously, that the world was an unsafe place and people were, in fact, out to get her. As a result, all of the previously mentioned symptoms, especially the hyper-vigilance and extreme anxiety, dominated her life, especially when out in public. These third cluster symptoms are often difficult to release because people feel safer with armed guards around them when they perceive a dangerous situation. Small children, for instance, prefer their parents around in public typically because their fears of unknown people and places are considerable. Teenagers, conversely, have figured out that parents are more of a nuisance than protection in those situations. So Marsha figured hyper-vigilance was the mindset of choice for her in a dangerous world because what if she let her guard down and something terrible happened again?

The answer to her dilemma, as I see it, is very similar to the mindset practiced by drivers after an automobile accident: caution is wise but living (driving) in "white knuckled" anxiety is self-destructive and makes for a most anxious and unhappy life. (We will re-visit this later in Sara's story.)

Okay, back to our friend, the middle toe. The third cluster translates into doing something protective, like wearing bigger shoes that won't rub against the injury or walking less or with a limp. Essentially, employing any technique necessary to protect the toe/foot from any further injury. Isn't this akin to avoidance, the second cluster? Yes, absolutely. As noted by trauma expert and renowned psychologist, Dr. Charles Whitfield, the mind is attempting to do two conflicting operations at the same time: remove the trauma by pushing it to the surface and bury the trauma by shoving it deep into the hardware of the mind.[4] And so it is with the splinter. All symptoms of PTSD are essentially a battle with these same operations: heal the trauma vs. bury it from all conscious thought!

The True Story of Sara

The following story is a true-to-life account written by a PTSD survivor, Sara, and used with her generous permission to do so.

Sara
"Overcoming Trauma and PTSD"

When I was in my mid 20's, I met a man that I eventually dated for about a year. Because of some circumstances, he opted to move five states away and we lost contact with one another. Then in my late 30's, I decided to look him up on Facebook, sent him a message, and we picked up our relationship where it had left off a decade earlier. Our newly re-established friendship soon turned serious and we began to talk about a future together and the option of my relocating closer to where he was living. We were both very excited about this new adventure in our lives and what the future had in store for us. I trusted him like no other man I had ever been with, so much that I gave him a key to my house so he could come and go as he pleased. I shared with him my every thought from daydreams to my deepest fears. I loved how comfortable it felt to be with him. We were so connected; I knew my life would never be the same. Little did I know how true that would be.

Another piece of the puzzle in my challenge was that this man was a master manipulator. As I was becoming reacquainted with him, I asked him if it would be okay to converse with some of his friends in the area in which he was living, in an effort to get to know another side of this "old friend stranger" whom I hadn't seen or spoken to in many years. He was more than agreeable to this. He provided me with email addresses to two of his closest friends with whom I began to converse. One of his friends had a girlfriend with whom I also conversed. I developed a good friendship with each of these three people via the internet, by way of email and instant messaging. What I later learned, was that this sociopath fabricated all these people for me to converse with, and they were all fake identities. HE was actually portraying all three of these people. He used these three other "people" to further learn ways to control, manipulate, and attack me.

One winter night, just a few months after I had relocated my life to be closer to him, I awoke to a knife-wielding, masked man at my bedside. He stabbed me 14 times at various points on my body. I pleaded with him to leave. "Please, sir. Please go. Please leave," I begged over and over again. But he would not leave. In fact, he remained in my house for two hours, attempting to strangle me with a bed sheet, torturing me, and holding me hostage. He zip-tied my ankles and wrists and forced me to lay face down in the hallway bleeding, naked, and left to die. Just before he left, he told me that I was not to move for two hours and that he would be waiting outside the door. If he saw any movement, he would come back in. I was terrified! After some time had passed, I found the courage to scoot myself to a nearby bathroom. I found some nail clippers and was able to cut the zip-ties on my ankles, but I couldn't maneuver the clippers enough to reach the ties on my wrists, due to the severe slashes sustained from blocking my face from the knife. I made my way to the kitchen and found scissors, walked back to my seat, placed the scissors between my knees, and somehow, was able to use my knees to get the scissors to cut the zip-ties off my wrists. I allowed more time to pass since I had no idea when he left or if he would return. It was now about four hours after the attack and the sun was about to rise. I knew I needed to call 911 but he had stolen my cell phone. Cautiously and with great fear, I went to the house next door and had them call for help. Police and rescue showed up and I was airlifted to a trauma hospital where my severe wounds could be tended to.

My parents were contacted and immediately flew out to me. After the necessary surgeries, I was discharged to the care of my parents. Three days after the attack, I returned to my house (the crime scene) to pack a few things to take with me, as I would be staying with my parents while I recuperated. I was adamant about finding a therapist to begin to help me overcome this horrific experience and to begin to heal. Within a few weeks, I would also have to decide if I would be moving back to my new residence. My initial challenges and fears were numerous, largely because my attacker had not yet been arrested. With the help of the detectives on the case, I was able to determine the identity of the attacker: of all people, it was the one man I trusted more than anything...the man I had become reacquainted with!

I found myself looking over my shoulder a lot, wondering if he was around somewhere. I would go out only for a couple of hours for a doctor's appointment or a therapy session, and was always accompanied by someone. I would want to come back to the safety of my parent's home immediately, no errands, no stopping for lunch. A family member even went as far as to cover every window on the lower level of my house so that I would be confident no one could see inside.

I was terrified of the dark and would sleep minimally. I wasn't afraid of falling asleep, but of opening my eyes to someone at the bedside once again. I wouldn't even sleep in a bedroom alone. I felt that I needed constant protection to keep me safe. Within a couple weeks of the attack, I received great news. The man had been found, arrested, and taken to jail with no bond. Immediately, a new sense of freedom overcame me. That would be the beginning of my return to normalcy. All the window coverings were removed that night, which was the first since the attack that I slept in a bedroom alone.

I remember one day being so emotionally overwhelmed that I laid on my bed for hours in the fetal position and sobbed, wondering if this was what my life was going to be like. Why me? What did I do to deserve such a thing? How dare he take my freedom and independence away! I found myself journaling on many occasions, especially on those sleepless nights. I was able to openly express many feelings of anger, hurt, resentment, sadness, and disbelief and, eventually, some level of acceptance of the situation. Journaling was one of the most therapeutic interventions to assist in my emotional healing.

The weeks that followed brought challenges as well as successes. I had a lot of uncertainty about staying up north to live versus moving back to my short-lived new home. I made the decision to return to the place I had recently began to call my home just a few months prior to live and make a fresh start. I was determined to not let that one person ruin my dream and continue to control all of my thoughts and actions. Now it was my time to be in control again—control of my own thoughts, actions, and life choices. Three months after the attack, I moved back to live on my own. I was terrified. I kept nearly every light on at my house all night long. Bit by bit, my confidence grew, and I found myself forgetting to leave all the lights on and the quest for normalcy began. My main goal was to take back control of my life.

Once I returned to my new house, I researched to find a therapist who specialized in PTSD. I knew I still had a lot of healing to do both physically and emotionally. I had many new fears that had to be faced so that I could re-gain my life and independence. I feared the dark, I feared living alone, I feared being attacked again. My overall trust for people was minimal. I wouldn't leave home after sunset. I wouldn't walk anywhere where someone couldn't see me. I wouldn't use a sharp knife, let alone purchase a new set (my old set was collected as evidence). I had irrational thoughts of someone being in my house and hiding in a place as small as a cupboard. I feared masks of any sort. My heart would pound with anxiety and fear whenever I would encounter any one of these fears.

With the help of my therapist I was able to successfully overcome many of the fears that had come about as a result of the attack. My therapist worked with me, using many different options to work through my fears. The use of self-talk was one such option. When something scared me, I learned to tell myself I was safe and that no one was going to hurt me. The night of the attack, the moon was full. I found myself being scared on subsequent months when the moon was full. My therapist helped me change my thought process from fearing the full moon to the light of the moon helping me to make it to my neighbors safely to call for help. My therapist stated, "The full moon is our friend. It lights our path." Years after the attack I still says that. One pivotal session was when he had me do an exercise in imagery. He asked me to close my eyes and relax. Once relaxed, he asked me to envision the attacker (as I knew him in the relationship) sitting there. I described how I would approach my attacker and tell him how I was feeling now, how I felt during the attack, and how angry I was at how, even after the attack, I still spent time and energy being fearful of so many things, and the impact his lies and deceit had on my current relationship. Toward the end of the session, I was able to say goodbye to him and let him know how worthless he is and that I would no longer allow him to take up my thoughts and my future stewing about what had happened. While I wasn't symptom free, that session made a huge difference in my progress toward overcoming that tragic event. I would gradually find myself staying out after dark and leaving fewer lights on at home. In addition, I became less neurotic about looking in every room in my house upon returning from any place I had gone out to.

Part of my recovery was found in educating others on the dangers of the internet and social networking sites. Attending and speaking at Victim's Rights events was also very therapeutic in the sense that it helped me find yet another positive in what some may consider to be a tragic event. One thing that my therapist told me was, "the worst day of your life can also be the best day of your life." Because of such opportunities to share and help others, I believe, wholeheartedly, that the night of my attack was one such instance.

Despite all the lies, deceit, and manipulation that I was subject to throughout the duration of my relationship with my attacker, I have once again learned to trust others and have even found love again. The occurrences of PTSD triggers are minimal and I continue to challenge myself with lingering fears in an effort to fully recover.

Today I continue to seek out opportunities to help keep others safe and to share my story in the hope that it will give others the strength to overcome whatever life's challenges may bring.

A 5-Step Plan for Healing

To be sure, Sara is an incredible person, courageous, persistent, and resilient (the flip side of which, according to Sean, her significant other, is "damned stubborn"). But Sara's story is not included here to extol her considerable virtues, but because she is every woman/every human. She could be you and you could be her. You could do what she did by employing that same courage and perseverance. But you would need a good game plan and a good therapist that you trusted with your soul.

So what do you need to triumph like Sara and so many others? To repeat myself, your clinician should understand trauma and how human beings heal from emotional wounds and psychological trauma. If they mention anything about time healing all wounds, run, don't walk, to the next trauma expert on your list. Time only passes; humans heal from emotional trauma by actively applying a five-step formula that works, consistently, when people present with the courage to resolvetheir issues.

I will recall the five-step process as it applies to Sara's case and also talk about the tools and power tools utilized. She began with the power tool of psychotherapy. Sara, and all others grappling with a trauma that is actively haunting the individual and dominating his or her life, should not attempt to take this healing project on without professional help. Experienced professionals have many stories of people who have championed their trauma and are no longer tormented by it. Some even have survivors that will talk to their prospective patients about their success. You would do at least that in trying out a new hairdresser.

Recovery from trauma is a process—the first part of which is building a safe rapport with your therapist. Only when *you* feel safe enough to proceed into the room(s) in your head with the skull and crossbones and *KEEP OUT* sign on the door, do you enter. Similarly, you move at a pace you can handle. No one else's pace matters. Think of a professional trainer who works out four hours a day. Your pace, not his. Sara worked quickly. She decided within only a couple of sessions that she could tell me anything and everything. She held back nothing from the traumatic account.

1. Remember

Remember, the first of the five steps requires a complete return to the trauma—recall the "A" word, of accepting the reality of the trauma and not avoiding, minimizing, or denying it.

Every detail of the traumatic memory must be included, because there is power in the details. Trauma survivors have had to return to "the scene of the crime," so to speak, because they omitted important details where they felt very frightened, shocked, sad, and/or hurt. Sara never liked talking about the gloves or the mask, as they added a "creepy" component to the story.

If, as in the case of the survivors of childhood sexual abuse, there are multiple accounts and traumas to share, every account has power and must be re-visited and worked through to completion. Healing one account out of many is a good way to start, but it is only that. The stories typically surface one at a time, as if candies in the Pez dispenser or cups in a cup dispenser. One memory is pulled down and shared to completion and then the next one appears, usually with no provocation on the part of either patient or therapist. Sara had only one trauma—albeit an ugly one—to champion, but to do so required remembering all aspects of it.

2. Feel

The second of the five steps for healing is to feel. Therapists should beware of people who can talk about their trauma rotely dry-eyed and devoid of emotion. PTSD is born out of *emotional* trauma. Even in cases where there is no physical danger, as in betrayal, abandonment, or fondling, your emotional trauma will simply not heal without feeling the original emotions, especially fear and hurt—to the fullest extent. Circumventing the feelings is tantamount to denial; it becomes a distant story that you can tell repeatedly with no resolution, because you never allow yourself the necessary exposure to the feelings. The power tool of deliberate exposure requires you to face your great fear, feel the feelings, and not resort to your self-destructive behavior (drinking, cutting, obsessive rituals, endless Facebooking). You combat veterans are not excluded; your PTSD symptoms won't go away if you vow to never tell your story and never shed a tear. Your toughness must be made manifest, not in running from the horrors of combat, but in offering yourself permission to feel all of your emotions. And then when you feel them, they must be expressed.

3. Express

Emotions that are felt but not expressed are stuck in psychological purgatory—they require a nudge to get to the promised land. Sara wrote extensively in a journal—another excellent garden tool—but even that wasn't enough. She needed to share her thoughts and feelings with me. The tears that patients are abhorrent to express are the very vehicle that transports them from darkness to healing absolutely anything. Sara allowed herself to get into the teeth of her emotional trauma, the abject horror of a masked man stabbing and stabbing at her in an attempt to end her life.

But her expressions didn't stop there; she had to tell me what it was like to discover that she had no cell phone, that it was necessary to crawl across the floor to the bathroom fearing that he would return, and then tell me what it was like to find out later that her perpetrator was indeed her boyfriend (try to imagine how that would feel, even for a minute).

All emotions must be expressed. A box of tissues is essential in the telling, because to unleash the memory is to tap into and drain a deep reservoir of emotional pain that is the very essence of the above-mentioned PTSD symptoms.

There is an important omission that survivors may require some prompting to express: very often after a rare, childhood molestation or physical assault there is a warning issued from perpetrator to survivor. "Never tell anyone what happened here today, or..." The threats are often as despicable as the offense and all of it promotes the trauma symptoms and the secrecy that so often follows. But now you have a therapist and you need to tell the tale in detail. Every bloody bit of it.

4. Release

The expression of emotion is curative, if it is released. That is, let go. Crying over the death of your loved one provides relief at the moment, but to achieve genuine peace regarding that loss, your loved one must be released. You must accept that she or he is gone and not coming back and somehow that is okay. Easy to say, excruciatingly painful to do.

Sara's release was about letting go of the horrible trauma so that she no longer needed to see it, feel it, or revisit it. But there was more to release: she had to release her protective suspicion and hyper-vigilance alluded to above. That is, she needed to "talk back to herself" when she wanted to say, "all men are not to be trusted, they will deceive you and try to kill you in the end." In fact, to trust Sean (the new man) she needed to release the perpetrator and put him in a category of sick, demented men, not every man or, of course, she would never let another man near her.

This is where the power tool of guided imagery was so helpful. I returned Sara to the scene—she watched from a seat in an imaginary movie theater so she could witness the horrible attack one more time. She was instructed to finish every aspect of the incident on the screen and then enter the movie at the end to minister to herself, providing love, support, and hope to the fallen Sara.

Even that wasn't enough: Sara needed to speak directly to the perpetrator, one last time, to express and release all of the hurt and rage she held since the night of the attack. Why not keep it? Because resentment and hate are toxins, poisons that will only serve to contaminate Sara's life and all future relationships. To release the attacker is to dismiss him from the driver's seat of her life and reduce him to a small part in the movie of her life. The goal, ultimately, is to take the worst scene in her life and morph it into the impetus for the very best changes Sara could make. Sara is healthier today than she was before the incident, not because of the attack, but because of the work she did to heal and grow afterward.

5. Think Differently

Live your beliefs and you can turn the world around.

—Henry David Thoreau

Let me begin the fifth stage by stating that it is not the fifth and final state at all, but is a part of every stage from the moment therapy begins until the last day of life. Thinking differently incorporates every cognitive tool explained in Chapters 4 and 5, from focus = energy to cognitive restructuring. You must think well to be well.

Remember investment plus threat = anxiety? Sara knew that healing meant to release the notion of threat, which doesn't belong in all aspects of life, the streets in town, her apartment, and the anniversary of the attack. Sara needed to replace her fear-based thoughts with more realistic ones: "Sean is not a perpetrator; there is no magic in a certain date on the calendar; mine is a safe neighborhood; I can love again without fear of attack; I am strong and can deal with whatever is ahead for me in life; I am a survivor and a victor."

The need to think differently permeates all aspects of any survivor's life. Just hearing from a therapist, "It's not your fault," is a huge contribution. (Of course it's not enough, because the other four stages are essential for healing.) So are other important cognitive "reframes" including, "I can do this; I can choose the attitude I want; one crazy/sick person doesn't get to write the script for my life; I can find meaning in my suffering and trauma; I will learn from this and use my learning to help others; I have plenty of love and support in my life; I am courageous and capable of healing…"Add your own self statements here.

Most importantly, always believe that, above all, there is hope, and with hope, healing.

> According to research, you are more likely to suffer symptoms of PTSD by a trauma induced by humans (incest) than nature causes (a hurricane). The most common cause of PTSD? Automobile accidents.[5]

Take Home Messages:

1. PTSD is the result of a traumatic experience where you survive but life is never the same.

2. Intrusive re-experiencing of the trauma, or bits and pieces of it, defines the first cluster of symptoms.

3. Avoiding situations or circumstances that may invoke memories of the traumatic event defines the second cluster of symptoms.

4. Being hypervigilant or always feeling on edge defines the third cluster of PTSD symptoms. Because the behaviors associate with this cluster lead to a sense of increased security, this may be the most difficult cluster of symptoms to work through.

5. Time only passes. Healing is an active process that requires remembering, feeling, expressing, releasing, and thinking differently.

Exercises

1. Tracking your experiences related to PTSD symptoms can be helpful for you and your therapist. Items to take note of include the event that seems to have been the trigger, the emotional feeling and its intensity, what you may have automatically believed about the event, and what you believe about the event looking back at it. If you are not experiencing many triggers, this exercise is also effective in using the intrusive images that you have experienced in the past.

2. Practice the tools from Chapter 4—especially those related to breathing and mindfulness. Being able to lower your anxiety level willfully with your breathing is a surprisingly powerful tool and will be helpful not only for the therapeutic process but forever. As well, you may find that mindfulness-based meditations that are "grounding," present, and tactile to be especially helpful as it offers a way to become immediately aware of the present moment, the smells around you, the texture of your pants, the (ideally) calming sounds of nature quietly providing a soundtrack for the moment, and whatever else you can experience with all of your senses here and now.

onclusion

You're on your own. And you know what you know,
and you are one who'll decide where to go.

—Dr. Seuss

When I was a kid, we had an annual family tradition of decorating the faux Christmas tree with the bent branches and not-very-convincing white pine needles. We would also make piping hot chocolate with a variety of Christmas cookies to share, before gathering to watch the holiday specials, including Charlie Brown, the Grinch, and my favorite, Rudolph the Red-Nosed Reindeer.

The Rudolph cartoon featured the "Abominable Snowman," the stuff of childhood nightmares: fangs, claws, and an appetite for destruction. But we were relieved when Hermie, the elf who was a Pell Grant shy of dental school, de-fanged and de-clawed the beast. The heart-warming transition culminated in Abominable becoming a gentle giant, and famously placing the angel atop the monstrous Christmas tree.

As a psychologist, I get to watch this story play out repeatedly in the lives of my patients. For instance, the scary step-mother from your night-marish childhood, menacing fangs, claws, and debilitating insults, threatens to once again destroy your confidence as a young man. Instead, you establish a boundary for the very first time and refuse to be dominated and controlled. The abusive mom has at last lost her power to evoke the horrible feelings of anxiety that represented your self-doubt and fear of failure.

Anxiety is defeated (or at least well-managed) on a daily basis by brave people everywhere: you could drop out of the class that requires the presentation, but instead you practice hours in front of the mirror, your mother, your cat (until Muffy could also give the presentation), and then knock it out of the park!

Perhaps your husband is gone for good this time and, quite frankly, that is probably for the best after all the cheating, drinking, and violence. You've considered suicide, but how is that an option when you see those precious, twin, 5-year-old faces that so depend on you? You know that you are not the first single mother to venture out alive. You decide that these kids deserve the best you have, so you turn your anxiety into passion: you work, pick up your girls, do homework, and sing songs together. And then, after you read them *I Love You, Stinky Face*, you muster up the strength to do online classes until you drop. Your girls have a role model for life. It's you, the terrified mother who wouldn't succumb to her anxiety.

Are you the guy with Parkinson's who continues to golf even with debilitating tremors? The breast cancer survivor who proudly shaves her head when the hair falls out? The widower who continues to volunteer your time for the Down's Syndrome residents?

Anxiety is a lifeforce to be reckoned with. Its voice echoes in your mind, repeating phrases like "you'll never make it," "you're not smart enough, tall enough, pretty enough, skilled enough, good enough, white enough." You can listen if you want. You can give up, drop out, drown your anxiety, drug your panic, and retreat into a safe, comfortable non-challenging life. You can spend your time watching other people live their lives on TV and the Internet, because you have no life to live.

But I have a challenge for you. How about you take up dancing, macramé, water skiing, yoga, softball, join a service club, write your memoirs, get a massage, get a license to massage, get a tandem bike (and then someone to ride with), get a kayak (and then someone to row with), learn an instrument, deliver food to shut-ins, take a comedy class and then show up on "open mic night," visit a nursing home with your guitar, make some soup for a sick person, practice mindfulness until there is no tomorrow, get a good therapist and start to recover from that rape, divorce, or molestation, learn to swim, teach a child to swim, join a gym, run a marathon, learn to surf, and accept everything you can't change, fix, or control.

Anxiety is an energy. Learn to use it to make the world a better place. Because, in the end, the beast has no more fangs than what you allow him.

Chapter Notes

Introduction
1. Alice Park. "The Two Faces," 2011.
2. R. Kessler et al., "Epidemiology of anxiety disorders," 21–35.

Chapter 1
1. J. Ormel et al., "Common mental disorders," 1741–1748.
2. "Anxiety Disorders," *www.bmawellness.com/psychiatry/anxiety_disorders.html*
3. R. Carlson, *Don't Sweat the Small Stuff...and It's All Small Stuff.* (New York: Hyperion, 1997).

Chapter 2
1. R. Sladky et al., "Disruptive Effective Connectivity," 10:1093/cercor/bht279.
2. David King, personal interview, 2014.
3. Dr. Cathy Frank, "How Is 'Normal' Anxiety," *http://abcnews.go.com/AnxietyOverview*

Chapter 3
1. M. Nadeem, "Impact of anxiety," 519–528.
2. T. Holmes, "The social readjustment rating scale," 213–21.
3. Holmes and Rahe brought to light that stress is not just caused by negative events in one's life, but also positive events.

4. *www.oprah.com/health/Sensory-Deprivation-Chamber-Stress-Relief*

5. K.S. Kendler, "Lifetime prevalence, demographic risk," 1022–1031.

Chapter 4

1. P.B. Polatin et al, *Spine*, 66–71.

2. Gary Emery and J. Campbell. *Rapid Relief from Emotional Distress.* (New York: Random House Publishing Group, 1987).

3. M.J. Kim, "The Structural Integrity," 37.

4. Dr. Daniel Levitin, "Discovered through a meta-analysis."

5. With due respect to Groucho Marx, I would gladly belong to any group he belonged to except the group of already deceased people.

6. "Myth-Conceptions," or Common Fabrications, Fibs, and Folklore About Anxiety, *Anxiety and Depression Association of America.*

7. Kathleen Romto, *Stress Management.* (Healthwise, Inc., 2013).

8. Mayoclinic.com, "Depression and Anxiety," 2008.

9. J. Burns, "The effect of meditation," 132–144.

10. Ibid.

11. Proverbs 3:5:6; Matthew 6:14 and 15; Matthew 6:26-34; Jeremiah 30:17; 1 John1:9; 1 John 2:25; John 17:3; John 3:16; 1 Peter 5:10.

12. Viktor E. Frankl, *Man's Search for Meaning*: New York, 2006.

Chapter 5

1. Are they any reasons or people where Guided Imagery is not appropriate? If people have suffered from psychotic symptoms, especially hallucinations, imagery may not be the best choice of treatments. If people are incapable of visualization, the technique is unlikely to work.

2. Nancy E. Richeson, "Effects of Reiki on Anxiety," 2010.

3. S. Barker, "The effects of animal-assisted therapy," *http://journals. psychiatryonline.org/article.aspx?articleid=81469*

4. J. Sanchez-Meca, "Psychological treatment of panic disorder," 37–50.

5. Andrew Weil. "Wellness Therapies," *www.drweil.com/drw/u/ ART03176/Qigong-Dr-Weils-Wellness-Therapies.html*

6. Tammy McIlvanie, "Massage and Anxiety," Personal correspondence. (June 12, 2014).

7. H. Benson, *The Relaxation Response.* (New York: William Morrow and Company, 1975).

8. E. Jacobson, *Progressive Relaxation,* 1938.

9. F. Pagnini, "A brief literature review," 71-81.

10. E. Jacobson, *Progressive Relaxation,* 1938.

11. Eckhart Tolle, *The Power of Now.* (Novato, Calif.: New World Library, 2004).

12. B. Smith, "A pilot study comparing," 251–258.

13. Ibid.

14. Daniel Wegner, *The White Bear Story,* Department of Psychology, Rice University.

15. Dr. Mehmet Oz, *Yoga Unveiled.* (2004).

16. J. Creswell, "Brief mindfulness meditation training," 1–12.

Chapter 6

1. S.L. Murphy, "Deaths: Final Data for 2010."

2. O. Doehrmann, "Predicting Treatment Response in Social," 87–97.

3. Palacios Gracia, et. al., "Comparing Acceptance and Refusal Rates," 722–724.

4. L. Reuterskiold, "Fears, Anxieties and Cognitive-Behavioral," 1–7.

Chapter 7

1. Kurt Kroenke, "Anxiety Disorders in Primary Care," 317–325.

2. W.M. Comptom, "Prevalence, correlates, disability and comorbidity," 566–576.

Chapter 8

1. Dominque Guel, " Neuronal correlates of obsessions," 557–562.

2. J. Abramowitz, et al., "The Effectiveness of Treatment," 55–63.

3. J. Nadeau, *Effective Management of OCD,* 2014.

Chapter 9

1. S. Segal, "How Stress Hormones Promote."

2. "Generalised anxiety disorder and panic disorder (with or without agoraphobia) in adults: Management in primary, secondary, and community care—guidance" (CG113). National Institute for Health and Care Excellence. (2011)

3. E. Kross, "Facebook Use Predicts Decline," doi: 10/1371/journal. pone.0069841

4. A. Loes et al "Origin of the Comorbidity," 39–49

5. Timothy A. Brown, "Current and Lifetime Comorbidity," 585–599; F. Lamers, "Comorbidity patterns of anxiety," 341–348.

6. "Mental Health and Substance Abuse-Related," *AHRQ-HCUP Statistical Brief* 92 (2010).

7. M. Kanamori, "A day care program," 234–239.

Chapter 10

1 *Diagnostic and Statistical Manual of Mental Disorders, DSM-IV-TR, Fourth Edition*. Washington, D.C.: American Psychiatric Association, 2000.

2. U.S. Department of Veterans Affairs (*www.ptsd.va.gov/public*), 2013.

3. William Schlenger, PhD, "Long-Term Course of PTSD," *Medscape www.medscpare.com/viewarticle/829872*

4. Whitfield, C. "Adverse childhood experience," 361–364.

5. Blanchard, E. and E. Hickling. *After the Crash: Psychological Assessment and Treatment of Survivors of Motor Vehicle Accidents (second ed.)*. Washington, D.C.: American Psychological Association, 2003.

Bibliography

Abramowitz, J. et al., "The Effectiveness of Treatment for Pediatric Obsessive-Compulsive Disorder: A Meta- Analysis," *Behavior Therapy* 36 (2005): 55–63.

"Anxiety Disorders," Behavioral Medicine Associates Comprehensive Modern Mental Health Services. *www.bma wellness.com/ psychiatry/anxiety_disorders.html*

Aubele, T., S. Wenck, and S. Reynolds, *Train Your Brain to Get Happy.* Avon, Mass.: Adams Media, 2011.

Barker, S. and K. Dawson, "The effects of animal-assisted therapy on anxiety ratings of hospitalized psychiatric patients," Psychiatric Services (1998). http://journals.psychiatryonline.org/article. aspx?articleid=81469

Benson, H., M.Z. Klipper. *The Relaxation Response.* New York: William Morrow and Company, 1975.

Blanchard, E. and E. Hickling. *After the Crash: Psychological Assessment and Treatment of Survivors of Motor Vehicle Accidents (second ed.).* Washington, D.C.: American Psychological Association, 2003.

Brown, Timothy A., Laura A. Campbell, Cassandra L. Lehman, Jessica R. Grisham, and Richard B. Mancill. "Current and Lifetime Comorbidity of the DSM-IV Anxiety and Mood Disorders in a Large Clinical Sample," *Journal of Abnormal Psychology*, 110 no. 4 (2001): 585–599.

Burdick, D. *Mindfulness Skills Workbook for Clinicians and Clients.* Eau Claire, Wis.: PESI Publishing and Media, 2013.

Burke, P., V. Meyer, S. Kocoshis, D. Orenstein, R. Chandra, D. Nord, J. Sauer, and E. Cohen, "Depression and anxiety in pediatric inflammatory bowel disease and cystic fibrosis," *Journal of the American Academy of Child & Adolescent Psychiatry, 28* no. 6 (1989): 948–951.

Burns, J., R. Lee, and L. Brown, "The effect of meditation on self-reported measures of stress, anxiety, depression, and perfectionism in college population," *Journal of College Student Psychotherapy* 25 (2011): 132–144.

Buscaglia, L. *Living Loving and Learning.* New York: The Ballentine Publishing Group, 1982.

Carlson, R. *Don't Sweat the Small Stuff...and It's All Small Stuff.* New York: Hyperion, 1997.

Chansky, T. *Freeing Your Child From Obsessive-Compulsive Disorder.* New York: Three Rivers Press, 2000.

Cloud, H. and J. Townsend. *Boundaries: When to Say Yes, How to Say No, to Take Control of Your Life.* Grand Rapids, Mich.: Zondervan Publishing, 1992.

Comptom, W.M., Y.F. Thomas, F.S. Stinson, B.F. Grant, "Prevalence, correlates, disability and comorbidity of DSM-IV drug abuse and dependence in the United States: results from the National Epidemiologic Survey on Alcohol and Related Conditions." *Archives of General Psychiatry,* 64 no. 5 (2007): 566–576.

Cortman, C. and H. Shinitzky, *Your Mind: An Owner's Manual for a Better Life.* Franklin Lakes, N.J.: The Career Press, Inc., 2010.

Cottraux, J. "Nonpharmacological treatments for anxiety disorders," *Dialogues in Clinical Neuroscience,* 4 no. 3 (2002).

Creswell, J., L. Pacilio, E. Lindsay, K. Brown, K. "Brief mindfulness meditation training alters psychological and neuroendocrine responses to social evaluative stress," *Psychneuroendocrinology* 44 (2014): 1–12.

Diagnostic and statistical manual of mental disorders (5th ed.). Arlington, Va.: American Psychiatric Publishing, 2013.

Doehrmann, O., S.S. Ghosh, F.E. Polli, G.O. Reynolds, F. Horn, A. Keshavan, C. Triantafyllou, Z.M. Saygin, S. Whitfield-Gabrieli, S.G. Hofmann, M. Pollack, J.D. Gabrieli, "Predicting Treatment Response in Social Anxiety Disorder from Functional Magnetic Resonance Imaging." *JAMA Psychiatry* 70 (2013): 87–97.,

Dyer, W. *The Power of Intention: Learning to Co-Create Your World Your Way.* New York: Hay House, Inc., 2010.

Emerson, R.W. *The Selected Writings of Ralph Waldo Emerson.* New York: The Penguin Group, 1965.

Emery, G., and J. Campbell. *Rapid Relief from Emotional Distress.* New York: Random House Publishing Group, 1987.

"Exercising to relax." February 2011. Harvard Men's Health Watch. *www. health.harvard.edu/newsletters/Harvard_Mens_Health_Watch/2011/ February/exercising-to-relax* [who wrote this?]

Fauci, Anthony S., et al. *Harrison's Principles of Internal Medicine, 17th ed.* New York: McGraw-Hill Professional, 2008.

Frank, C. "How Is 'Normal' Anxiety Different From An 'Anxiety Disorder'?" *http://abcnews.go.com/Health/AnxietyOverview/ story?id=4659631.* November 20, 2008.

Frankl, Viktor E. *Man's Search for Meaning.* New York: Beacon Press, 2006

Fremont, W. "School refusal in children and adolescents," *American Family Physician,* 68 no. 8 (2003).

Gracia, Palacios, et, al. "Comparing Acceptance and Refusal Rates of Virtual Reality Exposure vs. In-vivo Exposure by Patients with Specific Phobias," *Cyberpsychology and Behavior* 10 (2007): 722–724.

Guel, D., A. Bennazzouz, B. Aouizerate, E. Cuny, J. Rotge, A. Rougier, J. Tignol, B. Bioular, and P. Burband. "Neuronal correlates of obsessions in the caudate nucleus," *Biological Psychiatry,* 63 (2008): 557–562,

Gunaratana, B. *Eight Mindful Steps to Happiness: Walking the Buddha's Path.* Sommerville, Mass.: Wisdom Publications, 2001.

Harrington, A. *The Cure Within.* New York: W.W. Norton & Company, Inc., 2008.

Hazlett-Stevens, H. *Psychological Approaches to Generalized Anxiety Disorder.* Springer eBooks, 2008.

Hofmann, S, A. Sawyer, A. Witt, and D. Oh. "The effect of mindfulness-based therapy on anxiety and depression: A meta-analytic review," *Journal of Consulting Clinical Psychology,* 78 no. 2 (2010): 169–183.

Holmes, T. and R. Rahe. "The social readjustment rating scale," *Journal of Psychosomatic Research* 11 no. 2 (1967): 213–21.

Jacobson, E. *Progressive Relaxation.* Chicago: University of Chicago Press, 1938.

James, W. *The Principles of Psychology* 2 (1890): 449–50.

Kanamori, M., M. Suzuki, K. Yakamoto, M. Kanda, E. Kojima, H. Fukawa, T. Sugita, T. H. Oshiro. "A day care program and evaluation of animal-assisted therapy (AAT) for the elderly with senile dementia," *American Journal of Alzheimer's Disease and Other Dementias*, 16 no. 4 (2001): 234–239.

Kendler, K.S., T.J. Gallagher, J.M. Abelson, and R.C. Kessler. "Lifetime prevalence, demographic risk factors, and diagnostic validity of nonaffective psychosis as assessed in a US community sample," *Archive of General Psychiatry* 53 (1996): 1022–1031.

Kessler, R., A. Ruscio, K. Shear, H. Wittchen. "Epidemiology of anxiety disorders," *Current Topics in Behavioral Neurosciences,* 2 (2010): 21–35.

Kim, M.J. and P.J. Whalen. "The Structural Integrity of an Amgydala-Prefrontal Pathway Predicts Trait Anxiety, the Journal of Neuroscience," 29 no. 37 (2009).

King, David. Personal interview, 2014.

Kroenke, Kurt, MD; Robert L. Spitzer, MD, Janet B.W. Williams, DSW; Patrick O. Monahan, PhD; and Bernd Lowe, MD, PhD, "Anxiety Disorders in Primary Care: Prevalence, Impairment, Comorbidity and Detection, Annals of Internal Medicine," 146 no. 5 (2007): 317–325.

Kross, E. "Facebook Use Predicts Decline in Subjective Well-Being in Young Adults," PLoS One 8. doi: 10/1371/journal.pone.0069841

Lamers, F., P. van Oppen, et. al. "Comorbidity patterns of anxiety and depressive disorders in a large cohort study: the Netherlands Study of Depression & Anxiety (NESDA)," *Journal of Clinical Psychiatry* 72 no. 3 (2011): 341–348.

Leahy, R. *The Worry Cure: Seven Steps to Stop Worry from Stopping You.* New York: Three Rivers Press, 2005.

Levitin, Dr. Daniel J., and Dr. Mona Lisa Chanda. "Discovered through a meta-analysis of 400 studies that...neuroscience of music at McGill University in Montreal." *Trends in Cognitive Sciences* (2013).

Loes, A. Marquenie, Annemiek Schade, Anton J.L.M van Balkom, Hannie C. Comjis, Ron de Graaf, Wilma Volleberg, Richard van Dyck, Wilm van den Brink, "Origin of the Comorbidity of Anxiety Disorders and Alcohol Dependence: Finding of a General Population Study," *European Addiction Research* (2007): 39–49.

Lydiard, R. "Worried Sick: Antidepressants as Anti-Inflammatory Agents," *PsychEd Up* 1 (2005): 12.

Mayoclinic.com "Depression and Anxiety: Exercise Eases Symptoms," *www.mayoclinic.org/diseases-conditions/depression/in-depth/depression-and-exercise/art-20046495,* 2008.

McIlvanie, Tammy. Massage and Anxiety, Personal correspondence, June 12, 2014.

"Mental Health and Substance Abuse-Related Emergency Department Visits Among Adults," *AHRQ-HCUP Statistical Brief* 92 (2007).

Meyer, V. "Modification of expectations in cases with obsessional rituals," *Behaviour Research and Therapy, 4,* 273-280, 1966.

Murphy S.L., Xu JQ, and KD Kochanek. "Deaths: Final Data for 2010." *National Vital Statistics Report, 61* (2013).

Nadeau, J. and E. Storch. *Effective Management of OCD: Findings and Recommendations.* 2014.

Nadeem, M., A. Ali, S. Maqbool, and S. Zaidi. "Impact of anxiety on the academic achievement of students having different mental abilities at university level in Bahawalpur (Southern Punjab) Pakistan," *International Online Journal of Educational Sciences, 4* no. 3 (2012): 519–528.

National Institute for Clinical Excellence. (2004). Management of anxiety in adults in primary, secondary and community care: Clinical Guideline 22. London: National Institute for Clinical Excellence.

NIMH: *What Is Anxiety Disorder? www.nimh.nih.gov/health/topics/anxiety-disorders/index.shtml.*

Nitschke, J., J. Sarinopoulos, D. Oathes, T. Johnstone, P. Whalen, T. Davidson, and N. Kalin. "Anticipatory activation in the amygdala and anterior cingulate in Generalized Anxiety Disorder and prediction of treatment response," *American Journal of Psychiatry,* 166 (2009): 302–310.

Ormel, J., M. VonKorff, T. Ustun, S. Pini, A. Korten, and T. Oldehinkel. "Common mental disorders and disability across culture," *JAMA* 272, no. 22 (1994): 1741–1748

Oz, M. *Yoga Unveiled: Evolution and Essence of a Spiritual Tradition* (DVD). Produced by Gita and Mukesh Desai, 2004.

Pagnini, F., G. Manzoni, G. Castelnuovo, and R. Molinari. "A brief literature review about relaxation therapy and anxiety," *Body Movement and Dance in Psychotherapy,* 8 no. 2 (2013). 71–81.

Park, Alice. "The Two Faces of Anxiety." *Time Magazine,* December 5, 2011.

Parsons, T. and A. Rizzo. "Affective outcomes of virtual reality exposure therapy for anxiety and specific phobias: A meta-analysis," *Journal of Behavior Therapy and Experimental Psychiatry,* 39 (2008): 250–261.

Pennebaker, J., J. Kiecolt-Glaser, and R. Glaser. "Disclosure of traumas and immune function: Health implications for psychotherapy," *Journal of Consulting and Clinical Psychology,* 56 no. 2 (1988): 239–245.

Perls, F., R. Hefferline, and P. Goodman, P. *Gestalt Therapy: Excitement and Growth in the Human Personality.* Gouldsboro, Maine: The Gestalt Journal Press, Inc., 1994.

Polatin P.B., R.K. Kinney, R.J. Gatchel, et al. *Spine* 18 no. 1 (1993): 66–71.

Richeson, PhD, CTRS, Nancy E.; Judith A. Spross, PhD, RN, FAAN; Katherine Lutz, FNP, RN; and Cheng Peng, PhD. "Effects of Reiki on Anxiety, Depression, Pain, and Physiological Factors in Community-Dwelling Older Adults," *Research in Gerontological Nursing,* 3 No. 3, (2010).

Reuterskiold, L. "Fears, Anxieties and Cognitive-Behavioral-Treatment of Specific Phobias in Youth," *Behaviour Research and Therapy* 27 (2009): 1–7.

Romto, Kathleen, and David Sproule. *Stress Management*. New York: Healthwise, Inc. 2013.

Sanchez-Meca, J., A. Rosa-Alcazar, F. Marin-Martinez, and A. Gomez-Conesa. "Psychological treamtnet of panic disorder with or without agoraphobia: A meta-analysis," *Clinical Psychology Review*, 30 (2010): 37–50.

Schlenger, PhD, William, "Long-Term Course of PTSD Revealed." *Medscape. www.medscpare.com/viewarticle/829872*

Segal, S. and Cahill, L., "How Stress Hormones Promote Brain's Building of Negative Memories," *Science Daily* 23 (2014).

Seligman, M. *Learned Optimism*. New York: Knopf, 1990.

Seligman, M. *What You Can Change And What You Can't: The Complete Guide to Successful Self-Improvement*. New York: Fawcett Books, 1993.

Seuss, Dr. *Oh, the Places You'll Go!* New York: Random House Children's Books, 1960.

Sladky, R., A. Hoflich, M. Kublbock, C. Kraus, P. Baldinger, E. Moser, R. Lanzenberger, and C. Windischberger. "Disrupted Effective Connectivity Between the Amygdala and Orbitofrontal Cortex in Social Anxiety Disorder During Emotion Discrimination Revealed by Dynamic Causal Modeling for fMRI," *Cerebral Cortex*. doi: 10.1093/cercor/bht279, 2013.

Smith, B., B. Shelley, J. Dalen, K. Wiggins, E. Tooley, and J. Bernard. "A pilot study comparing the effects of mindfulness-based and cognitive-behavioral stress reduction," *The Journal of Alternative and Complementary Medicine*, 14 no. 3 (2008): 251–258.

Snider, L. and S. Swedo. "Pediatric Obsessive-Compulsive Disorder," *The Journal of the American Medical Association*, 284 (2000): 3104–3106.

Sokolowska, E. and I. Hovatta. "Anxiety genetics—findings from cross-species genome-wide approach," *Biology of Mood & Anxiety Disorders*, 3 (2013): 9.

Stein, M., A. Simmons, J. Feinstein, and M. Paulus. "Increased amygdala and insula activation during emotion processing in anxiety-prone subjects," *American Journal of Psychiatry,* 164 (2007): 318–327.

Tolle, E. *The Power of Now: A Guide to Spiritual Enlightenment.* Novato, Calif.: New World Library, 2004.

Weil, A. *Natural Health, Natural Medicine: A Comprehensive Manual for Wellness and Self-Care.* New York: Houghton Mifflin Company, 1998.

Whitfield, C. "Adverse childhood experience and trauma American Journal of Preventive Medicine 14 no. 4 (1998): 361–364.

Yapko, M. *Suggestions of Abuse.* New York: Simon & Schuster, 1994.

Yerkes, R.M., and J.D. Dodson. "The relation of strength of stimulus to rapidity of habit-formation," *Journal of Comparative Neurology and Psychology,* 18 (1908): 459–482.

Young, E., J. Abelson, and O. Cameron. "Effect of comorbid anxiety disorders on the hypothalamic-pituitary-adrenal axis response to a social stressor in major depression," *Biologic Psychiatry, 56* (2004): 113–120.

Index

A

admission, mastering the skill of, 91

adrenaline, the brain and, 20

agoraphobia, 140-141

ambiguous roles, the perception of, 51-52

amygdala, anxiety and the, 19-20

anticipatory guidance, 74-76

arousal, PTSD and increased, 187-188

athletes, visualization and, 125-126

avoidance,
    counterproductive behaviors and, 21-22
    failure and rejection and, 30-31
    panic attacks and, 149
    phobias and, 127-137
    taking control of, 90-92

B

behavior, OCD and the importance of, 158

boundaries and communication, 72-73

brain, anxiety and what happens to the, 19-21

breathing,
    panic attacks and, 150
    the importance of, 86-87

C

challenges, growth and meeting, 32

change, the perception of, 49

closure, human beings and, 56

cognitions and emotions, relationship between, 146

cognitive
    exercises, worry and, 177
    restructuring exercises, phobias and, 132

About the Authors

Dr. Christopher M. Cortman has been a Florida Licensed Psychologist since 1985, and has now facilitated more than 60,000 hours of psychotherapy. Additionally, he has consulted for several local hospitals, law enforcement, and media. A popular speaker, Dr. Cortman has spoken alongside Tipper Gore (2009), Jane Pauley (2011), and is slated to appear with Patrick Kennedy in 2015. Dr. Cortman coauthored *Your Mind: An Owner's Manual for a Better Life* with Dr. Harold Shinitzky. Together, the tandem also created "The Social Black Belt," an evidence-based prevention/wellness curriculum for youth. Dr. Cortman also appeared on Radio Disney and co-hosted the radio show, "Your Mind Matters." He is the proud father of three children.

Dr. Harold Shinitzky was on the faculty at the Johns Hopkins University School of Medicine. He has been a Licensed Psychologist for more than 20 years. He specializes in Sports Psychology and works with Olympians and athletes from every professional association. He was the recipient of the Florida Psychological Association Distinguished Psychologist Award, the Outstanding Contributions to Psychology Award and the recipient of the Martin Luther King, Jr. Award for Community Service.

He is the coauthor of *Your Mind: An Owner's Manual for a Better Life*. Together they have converted *Your Mind* into an evidence-based, youth prevention curriculum titled "The Social Black Belt." They also co-hosted the radio show "Your Mind Matters." Dr. Shinitzky has been the Mental Health Correspondent for ABC Tampa and Baltimore, Animal Planet's *Fatal Attractions*, and is a frequent contributor for FOX and Radio Disney.

 **Dr. Laurie-Ann O'Connor** has graduate degrees in both clinical and counseling psychology as well as post-doctoral certification as a trauma professional. She is also a Certified Literacy Trainer. Dr. O'Connor's writings have appeared in newspapers, professional trade magazines, and peer-reviewed journals. For her presentations, she was recognized as a Speaker for the U.N. for the Year of the Family. She has studied in both Canada and the United States and is currently located in Venice, Florida, where she works in private practice in association with Dr. Cortman. Most recently, she has been instrumental in assisting the move of the The Social Black Belt from an experience to an evidence-based youth wellness and prevention program.